# わかりやすい共同海損

海損精算人 中田 栄一
EIICHI NAKADA, Average Adjuster

A Clear Guide to General Average

保険毎日新聞社

## ◆はじめに◆

　2016年7月から2017年7月まで10回にわたって、保険毎日新聞に「わかりやすい共同海損」を連載しました。幸い連載は、海運・貿易関係者の皆さんに好評でしたが、すべて読んでいらっしゃらない方もおり、「いざ、共同海損」という時にお役に立てるよう、保険毎日新聞社のご厚意により、加筆、修正し、ハンディな1冊にまとめました。

　1983年に大学を卒業し、株式会社東京海損精算事務所（現東京マリンクレームサービス株式会社）に入社し、共同海損の精算業務を始めた当初、共同海損の仕組みを、わかりやすく解説した入門書がなく、苦労したのを覚えています。

　新聞連載は、入門者に、できるだけわかりやすく共同海損の仕組みを理解してほしい、との筆者の想いから執筆しました。

　さらに書籍化にあたり、共同海損に関する実務に対応できるように、英語での解説 A Clear Guide to General Average、1994年ヨーク・アントワープ規則対訳集、2016年ヨーク・アントワープ規則の英文テキスト、共同海損に関する万国海法会ガイドラインおよび共同海損専門用語集（和英・英和）を加えました。

　本書が、海運・貿易関係者の皆さんの安全な航海の指針の1つになれば、幸いです。

　最後に、執筆に際し、東京マリンクレームサービス株式会社前社長の爲季伸樹氏ならびに東京海上日動火災保険株式会社コマーシャル損害部専門部長の久保治郎氏より、多大なご助言をいただいたことに謝意を表します。

2018年12月

　　　　　　　　　　　　　　　　　　　　　　　　海損精算人　中田　栄一

# ◆目　次◆
[Table of contents]

はじめに

## Ⅰ　わかりやすい共同海損　❶

### 第1章　船乗りのことわざ「板子一枚下は地獄」── 2
- ① はじめに／2
- ② 損害が起きた時のための工夫（海上保険と共同海損）／2
- ③ そもそも、海損って何でしょう？／3
- ④ 共同海損精算人って、どんな職業？／4
- ⑤ 次章以降のご説明／5

### 第2章　ラグビーの精神「一人はみんなのために、みんなは一人のために」── 6
- ① 共同海損と天秤ばかり／6
- ② 共同海損は3,000年近い昔から現在までずっと続いてきた海の自然法／6
- ③ 共同海損の大まかな仕組み／7

　**トピックス1**　共同海損の分担利益と負担価額の算定方法・9

### 第3章　「サルサ♪　カリブの海賊」共同海損 ── 12
- ① サルサ♪とハバナ旧市街、そして、カリブの海賊／12
- ② 海賊と共同海損／13
- ③ 共同海損の基本原理／13
- ④ 最後に、カリブの海賊からの贈り物、冷えたモヒートはいかが／15

### 第4章　共同海損認容に関する2つの基本思想（共同の安全と航海の完遂）── 17
- ① ニューヨークの自由の女神像／17
- ② 共同海損認容に関する2つの基本思想／18
- ③ 共同海損の成立時点／20
- ④ 共同海損分担利益（共同海損行為の結果、救われた財産）／20
- ⑤ 共同海損負担価額（共同海損行為の結果、救われた財産の航海終了時における価額）／20
- ⑥ 最後にコーラで乾杯／21

### 第5章　どんな費用が共同海損に認められるのでしょうか ── 22
- ① イギリス人の生涯の師／22
- ② イギリス人は割り勘が嫌？／23
- ③ どんな費用が共同海損になるのでしょうか？／24
- ④ 最後は、アフタヌーンティの優雅なひとときを／26

## 第6章　どんな損害が共同海損に認められるのでしょうか ―― 27
　　1　冬の星座――オリオンのギリシャ神話／27
　　2　どんな損害が共同海損になるのでしょうか？／28
　　3　最後に、簡単な頭の体操をしましょう／30
　　　**設　例**　共同海損犠牲損害認容額も共同海損を分担することによって衡平になる・30

## 第7章　船主の共同海損宣言（貨物に共同海損の分担を求める手続き）―― 32
　　1　伝統の襷（たすき）をつなぐ駅伝の魅力／32
　　2　襷をつないだ大先輩と共同海損のバイブル／32
　　3　船主の共同海損宣言／33
　　4　貨物から後日の支払いを約束してもらうためのよりどころ――マリタイム・リーエン／34
　　5　貨物保険と共同海損の関係／35
　　6　襷をつなぐための新年の抱負／36
　　　**トピックス2**　共同海損の精算地・36
　　　**トピックス3**　GAサーベイの手配・37
　　　**トピックス4**　共同海損費用保険の付保・37

## 第8章　ヨーク・アントワープ規則（海上運送契約で合意された共同海損精算のよりどころ）―― 38
　　1　コンテナ2万個積み超大型コンテナ船の登場／38
　　2　ヨーク・アントワープ規則って、何？／39
　　3　1994年YARと2016年YARの主な相違点／41
　　4　今後の見通し／43

## 第9章　共同海損の基本形と代換費用 ―― 44
　　1　くまモンの生みの親／44
　　2　ベストな選択／45
　　3　共同海損の基本形／45
　　4　代船輸送された場合の具体例／46
　　　**トピックス5**　船貨不分離協定（Non-Separation Agreement）・48

## 第10章　共同海損の精算書作成とコンサルティング ―― 50
　　1　世界中の人たちがシェアできるもの／50
　　2　共同海損に関する万国海法会（CMI）ガイドライン／51
　　3　共同海損精算人のコンサルティング業務／51
　　4　事案のより良い解決のために対話が大切／52
　　5　共同海損精算書の作成、発行および決済／52
　　6　おわりに／53
　　　**トピックス6**　過失と共同海損の関係・54

## II  A Clear Guide to General Average ... 55

- Chapter 1  What is General Average, or GA? — 56
- Chapter 2  What is the general image of General Average? — 58
- Chapter 3  What should we do when the GA accident happens? — 61
- Chapter 4  When a cargo is not insured, the cargo owner may get involved in trouble. — 63
- Chapter 5  What kind of expenses can be allowed in General Average? — 65
- Chapter 6  Specific example of the substituted expenses — 68
- Chapter 7  What kind of losses can be allowed in General Average? — 70
  1. Damage done to the ship or the cargo by fire fighting operations / 70
  2. Damage done to the ship or the cargo as a result of salvage operations / 71
  3. Loss of the ship or the cargo as a result of cargo handling at the port of refuge / 72
  4. Loss of the ship or the cargo by re-stowing the cargo for the common safety / 72
- Chapter 8  What are York-Antwerp Rules? — 74
  1. Are YAR a convention or law? / 74
  2. Why are the shipowners and the cargo owners bound to YAR? / 74
  3. How have YAR been amended? / 75
  4. How are YAR composed of ? / 76
- Chapter 9  Major points of difference between YAR 1994 and YAR 2016 — 77
  1. Whether or not salvage remuneration will be allowed in GA / 77
  2. Commission and interest on general average disbursements / 79
  3. Time bar for coutributions to general average / 79
  4. Outlook / 80
- Chapter 10  The job and the roles of GA adjusters — 82
  1. Self-introduction as a GA adjuster / 82
  2. Practical experience is essential to become a GA adjuster / 82
  3. Let's look at the job and roles of GA adjusters / 83
  4. Let's look at what GA adjusters will do along with the developments of the ship's accident / 84
  5. GA adjusters' thought / 87

## III  1994年ヨーク・アントワープ規則対訳集
York-Antwerp Rules 1994
（1999年7月東京マリンクレームサービス株式会社発行） ... 89

## IV  2016年ヨーク・アントワープ規則
York-Antwerp Rules 2016 ... 143

| Ⅴ 共同海損に関する万国海法会ガイドライン<br>CMI Guidelines relating to general average | 157 |

| Ⅵ 共同海損専門用語集（和英・英和）<br>Technical terms on general average | 171 |

著者紹介 About the author・177

# I

# わかりやすい共同海損

# 第1章

# 船乗りのことわざ「板子一枚下は地獄」

## 1 はじめに

皆さん、「板子（いたご）一枚下は地獄」という船乗りのことわざをご存知でしょうか。穏やかな海を航行している船でも、天候が急変し嵐に遭い、船底にある1枚の板が外れたら沈没してしまいます。船乗りの仕事は、死の危険と隣り合わせという意味です。

1890年9月16日21時頃、日本への親善航海のために寄港したトルコの軍艦「エルトゥールル号」が和歌山県串本町の紀伊大島沖で猛烈な台風のために岩礁に激突、蒸気機関が爆発し2つに割れ沈没し、艦長以下587人が殉職。紀伊大島の島民たちの献身的な救助活動により乗員69人が助かり、生存者は救護の後、日本海軍の軍艦「比叡」と「金剛」に分乗し、翌年1月にオスマン帝国の首都イスタンブールに送り届けられました。この話は映画化され、2015年12月に日本・トルコ合作映画『海難1890』として公開されました。

2013年6月インド洋を航行中の大型コンテナ船の船体が真ん中から折れ、船体の前部と後部の2つに分かれた後も、数日間浮かんでいましたが、結局コンテナ4,300個もの貨物もろとも海没した事故をご記憶の方もいらっしゃるかもしれません。

いつの時代も航海は、危険を伴うものです。海上運送に携わる人たちは、長い間さまざまな危険を排除し、予防し、軽減する取組みを行うとともに、残念ながら船舶や貨物に損害が発生してしまった場合には、その損害をどのようにして埋め合わせ、または、関係者間で分配するかを考え続け、工夫し続けてきました。

## 2 損害が起きた時のための工夫（海上保険と共同海損）

その工夫の1つとして海上保険が生まれたことはご存知のとおりです。冒険貸借と呼ばれる契約が海上保険の前身と言われています。これは、船主が船舶を、または、荷主が貨物を担保に資金を借り入れ、船舶または貨物が安全に目的港に到着した場合には利息を付けて借入金を返済するが、航海が無事に完了しなかった場合には元本、

利息ともに返済義務を免れるという契約でした。冒険貸借は、12世紀から13世紀にはイタリア、フランス、スペインなどの地中海沿岸都市で盛んに行われるようになり、その後、種々形を変え、14世紀中頃から後半にかけてほぼ現代と同様な形の海上保険に整えられたと言われます。したがって、海上保険は700年くらいの歴史を持っていると言うことができます。

近代的保険が海上保険から始まるということは通説となっており、上記の海上保険の成立ちについては、皆さんも種々の参考書でお読みになったと思います。しかし、皆さんは、この海上保険よりもっともっと古い、海の損害分担の工夫があることをご存知でしょうか。それが「共同海損」です。共同海損は、船舶と貨物の双方を救うための損害を、救われた財産で、救われた価額に応じて案分して負担するという仕組みであり、3,000年近い昔から海の自然法として存在しています。共同海損の仕組みは、紀元前8世紀にフェニキア人によって最初に用いられ、6世紀の初頭にローマ帝国のユスティニアヌス法典に最初に記されたと考えられています。

そして、共同海損より2,300年ほど遅れて生まれた海上保険に、共同海損が、保険金支払いの対象の1つの重要な要素として採り入れられているのです。

## ③ そもそも、海損って何でしょう？

海損とは、海上保険の専門用語で、全損にならない海上損害（分損）を意味します。英語では"average"と言います。そうです、皆さんがご存知の「平均」または「平均的な」、「普通の」を表すaverageです。損害保険会社に就職し海上保険分野に配属された新入社員は、まずこの専門用語に驚くようです。海上保険の本場イギリスでさえも、海運や貿易の仕事に従事していない普通の人に共同海損（GA；General Average）の意味を尋ねても、わからないと思います。

イギリスの海損精算人の笑い話ですが、「私は海損精算人（average adjuster）です」と言ったら、「なんだ、たいしたことないんだね。ごく普通の（average）アジャスターか。優秀じゃないんだね」と言われたそうです。

保険ブローカー制度が一般的な英米、ヨーロッパ諸国では、通常ブローカーや船舶保険の幹事会社が依頼した損害検査員（サーベイヤー）が船舶の損害状況、損害原因および損害額を調査し、検査報告書を発行します。また、船主が委嘱した海損精算人が、船舶保険約款、法令、海上運送契約等に基づき、いくら保険金として船舶保険会社から損害をてん補してもらえるかを判断します。この海上保険金算定作業のことを、海損精算と言います。

江戸時代末期に福沢諭吉によってヨーロッパの保険制度が日本に紹介され、明治初期に海上保険の引受けが開始されました。当時欧米のように海損精算人という独立し

Ⅰ　わかりやすい共同海損

た職業がなかったため、海上保険会社が自ら、欧米の海損精算人のように船舶保険金支払額の算定も行う慣行が今なお続いています。

## ④　共同海損精算人って、どんな職業？

　ただし、共同海損の精算は、非常に専門性が高く、精算技能を修得するのにかなりの年月を要するため、日本でも世界でも、貨物を積載した船舶で大きな海難事故が発生した場合には、共同海損精算人という専門家に共同海損の精算を委嘱するのが普通です。

　私のいとこに脚本家がいますが、彼は資料や取材に基づき映画や番組の構想を練り、台本（シナリオ）を作り、映画や番組を制作（プロデュース）しています。共同海損精算人の仕事も、脚本家と似ている側面があるように思えます。事故発生当初に船主さんから相談を受け、共同海損になるとしたらどのようにしたらよいかについての今後の展開（シナリオ）を示し、航海関係者間の衡平な利害を調整する共同海損精算書を発行（プロデュース）します。

　数年前、『世界がもし100人の村だったら』[(1)]という本がベストセラーになりましたが、共同海損の精算はまさにそうです。現在実際に共同海損正式精算書を作成しているのは世界で100人ぐらい、私は、日本に3人しかいない共同海損精算人（GAアジャスター）の1人です。

　30数年前、大学2年生の時に海外・貿易に興味があり、サークルの先輩の紹介で海上保険契約研究のゼミに入ったことが縁で、1983年に東京海損精算事務所（現・東京マリンクレームサービス）に入社しました。7年間東京で実務経験を積んだ後に、ロンドンとニューヨークの大手海損精算事務所に派遣され、業界で有名な海損精算人の指導の下、ケーススタディを中心に海損精算実務を学び、その後東京に戻り、独り立ちして共同海損精算書を作成するようになりました。

　私が勤務している東京マリンクレームサービスは、1967年に設立されましたが、共同海損精算に関しては、1917年設立の日本精算事務所の業務ならびに人員を継承しており、100年を超える歴史を有しています。また1957年の日本海損精算人協会創立当初から日本精算事務所・東京マリンクレームサービスが事務局として協会活動を支援し、1998年7月から私が事務局を兼務しています。

---

(1)　池田香代子著＝C. ダグラス・ラミス翻訳『世界がもし100人の村だったら』（マガジンハウス、2001）。

## 5　次章以降のご説明

　先日、ある海上保険関係者のお客様に共同海損についてお話しする機会がありました。その際、お客様の社長様から国際貿易取引を支える海上運送について理解を深めることはきわめて重要であり、また、共同海損の仕組みを知ることによって、荷主としての海難事故への対応時にも、慌てることなく対応することができ、海上保険ならびにリスク管理にも役立つ、とのコメントをいただきました。まさにそのとおりだと思います。

　これから、皆さんに、できるだけ平易に肩の凝らない内容で、わかりやすく共同海損の仕組みをご案内していきたい、と思います。

# 第2章

# ラグビーの精神
# 「一人はみんなのために、みんなは一人のために」

## 1 共同海損と天秤ばかり

　2015年夏イギリスで開催されたラグビーワールドカップで、日本チームが強豪南アフリカに歴史的勝利を挙げ、日本でもラグビーが再び脚光を浴びています。五郎丸歩選手のゴールキックをする前の祈りのポーズが有名になりました。そして、もう一つ広く知られるようになったのが、ラグビーの精神である「一人はみんなのために、みんなは一人のために」"One for all, all for one." という有名な言葉です。

　実は、この言葉は、海上運送の世界にもそのまま当てはまります。第1章でご説明した3,000年近い昔から現在まで続いている共同海損という制度がまさにこの精神を反映しているのです。この制度は、みんなのために（船舶と貨物の共同の安全のために）犠牲になった損害をみんなで分かち合うというもので、時として非常に大きな危険を伴う海上運送において、残念ながら海難事故が発生し、船舶と貨物の両方を救うことができた場合に、航海を共にする船舶や貨物といった関係者間の公平な損害の負担方法を定めているものです。

　世界の海上保険の主要なマーケットの1つであるロンドンにイギリス海損精算人協会という海損精算人の業界団体があります。この協会は1869年に創設されました。ロゴマークは海を航行する帆船と天秤ばかりです。天秤ばかりは英語でbalanceと呼ばれますが、右と左のお皿に載せた重さが均衡しないとどちらかが下がってしまいます。右と左がちょうど均衡する（バランスがとれる）ように調整（アジャスト）した結果を記載したものが精算書（アジャストメント）、この調整を行う専門家が精算人（アジャスター）と呼ばれます。天秤ばかりは、被保険者と保険会社間の調整、船舶や貨物といった航海を共にする関係者間の利害調整を表しているのです。

## 2 共同海損は3,000年近い昔から現在までずっと続いてきた海の自然法

　それでは、共同海損の歴史を少しさかのぼってみましょう。共同海損は、第1章でご説明したとおり、紀元前に生まれた海の自然法で、海上保険よりもずっと前から

第2章　ラグビーの精神「一人はみんなのために、みんなは一人のために」

【1572年インド カルカッタのパノラマ画】

出典：Georg Braun と Franz Hogenbergs 地図帳

あった制度です。

　紀元前4世紀から3世紀にかけて隆盛を極めた地中海東部のロドス島ロード海法では、船舶が暴風雨に遭い転覆しそうな危険な状態になったときに、船舶の船脚（ふなあし）を軽減する目的で貨物を船外に投げ捨てたとき（これを「投荷」と言い、「なげに」と読みます）は、すべての関係者のために犠牲になった貨物は、すべての関係者が分担して償わなければならない、と規定していました。

　古代ギリシャやローマ時代、船主以外の他者の貨物を輸送する場合には、通信手段が未発達だったこともあり、船主と一緒に、荷主または荷主の代理人も交易船に上乗り（supercargo）として乗船しました。荒天に遭遇した際に、荷主、あるいはその代理人の了解を得たうえで、貨物の一部が船外に投棄され、船が無事仕向け港に着き航海が終了した時点で、船長が各荷主に犠牲になった貨物の損害について分担を求めました。これが、共同海損精算の始まりであり、原型と考えられます。

　貨物を船外に投げ捨てることにより船舶の浮力が増し、暴風雨の危難から逃れることができるということを世界中の国の人たちが経験的に承知していました。みんなのために犠牲になったものをみんなで償うという衡平の思想は人類普遍のもののようです。

## ③　共同海損の大まかな仕組み

　それでは、まず皆さんに共同海損の大まかなイメージをつかんでいただきたい、と思います。

　世界を航行する船舶やそれにより運ばれる貨物にかかわる共同海損の取扱いを定めた統一的な規則として、1994年ヨーク・アントワープ規則（York-Antwerp Rules 1994、略称YAR、以下同）が、船荷証券および用船契約等の海上運送契約において、

現在、最も広く採用されています。YARについては、後で詳しくご説明しますので、ここでは単に、世界中で実務的に広く利用されているYARという統一規則が存在するとのみご理解ください。

YAR A条は、共同海損を次のように定義しています。

「共同の航海団体を構成する財産を危険から守る意図をもって、共同の安全のために、故意にかつ合理的に、異常な犠牲を払い、または費用を支出した場合に限り、共同海損行為が成立する。」

それでは、どのような事故が共同海損になるのでしょうか。上述した共同海損の原型である「投荷」は現代ではあまり行われませんが、皆さんにわかりやすい具体例でご説明しましょう。

貨物を積載した船舶が航行中、衝突、座礁、火災などの海難事故に遭遇しました。このまま何もしなければ、船舶と貨物の両方とも沈没、全損となる危険な状態になったため、船舶と貨物を共同の危険から救う目的で、船主は救助業者に救助を依頼しました。

救助船が海難現場に到着し、本船の大まかな損傷状況を確認したうえで、最も近くにある安全な港（避難港と言います）に向けて本船の曳航を開始し、とりあえず本船は避難港に入港しました。その後、避難港で、仕向け港（目的港）までの航海を完遂するために必要な船舶の損傷修繕を施工して、本船は仕向け港に無事到着することができました。

このような場合に、本船と貨物を救うために支出された救助費、本船の避難港入港関連費用等が、共同海損になります。共同海損費用は、仕向け港における航海終了時点（本船からの貨物揚げ切り時点）における船舶と貨物の救われたそれぞれの金額[2]に応じて、案分して負担される[3]ことになります。

この例で、おぼろげに共同海損の仕組みがおわかりいただけたのではないでしょうか。「共同海損制度とは、どのようなものですか？」という質問を受けたときに、簡単にその仕組みを説明しようとすれば、「船舶と貨物等の両方を救うために要した費用や損害を、仕向け港における救われたそれぞれの金額に応じて同じ比率で分担し合う仕組み」と答えることができると思います。

共同海損になる費用や損害を認定し、関係者に案分する作業を、共同海損精算と呼びます。実際にはどのような精算になるのでしょうか、簡単な例でご説明しましょう。

たとえば、救助費等の共同海損として認められる費用が3億円、仕向け港における

---

[2] 共同海損を負担する基準になる金額で、共同海損負担価額と言います。
[3] 船舶、貨物等の救われた関係者が支払う金額を共同海損分担額と呼びます。

## 第2章 ラグビーの精神「一人はみんなのために、みんなは一人のために」

**図表1** 共同海損精算例

| 共同海損分担利益<br>(共同海損行為の結果<br>救われた財産) | 共同海損負担価額<br>(救われた金額) | 共同海損分担額<br>(分担する金額) |
|---|---|---|
| 船　　舶 | ¥600,000,000 | ¥180,000,000 |
| 貨　　物 | ¥400,000,000 | ¥120,000,000 |
| 合計金額 | ¥1,000,000,000 | (共同海損として認められた費用の総額)<br>¥300,000,000 |

共同海損分担率：30％

　航海終了時の船舶の正味到達価額（救われた金額）が6億円、貨物の正味到達価額が4億円とすれば、船舶と貨物はそれぞれ図表1のように共同海損を案分して負担（分担）します。

　少し専門的な説明でわかりにくかったかもしれませんが、これが共同海損の大まかなイメージです。

　本船船長の判断によって、共同の安全のためにあえて支出された救助費等の共同海損費用が、船舶、貨物等の救われた関係者によって、どのように共同海損として分担されるのか、また、共同海損分担額を算定する際の難解で似通った専門用語の違いをご理解いただければ幸いです。

　より大雑把な言い方をすれば、共同海損は、船舶と貨物を救うための費用や、損害、および航海を完遂するために必要な費用や損害を、航海終了時の価額に応じて、救われた財産で傾斜配分して「割り勘」する仕組みです。

　共同海損は、海上運送独自の古い制度で、派手さはありませんが、今なお航海を共にする貿易関係者間の衡平な（バランスのとれた）利害調整に効果的な役割を果たしており、船主、船舶管理会社、用船者、荷主、フォワーダーの皆さんにとって、けっして無縁なものではありません。

---

**トピックス1**　共同海損の分担利益と負担価額の算定方法

　共同海損を分担する利益と、共同海損負担価額の算定方法は以下のとおりです。

(1) 船　　舶

　航海終了時※（最終仕向け港で貨物を揚げ切った時点）の船舶の正体市場価額評価額
　（Sound Market Value）
　損傷修繕費を控除
　共同海損に認容された修繕費を加算
　正味到達価額（Net Arrived Value）

※貨物全量が仕向け港まで代船により輸送された場合は、避難港で代船から貨物全量を揚げ切った時点（船貨分離の時点）

(2) 燃料（バンカー）

航海終了時※の本船残油の価額
共同海損認容額を加算
共同海損負担価額

※貨物全量が仕向け港まで代船により輸送された場合は、避難港で代船から貨物全量を揚げ切った時点（船貨分離の時点）

(3) 危険にさらされた運賃

危険にさらされた運賃の金額
共同海損事故発生後、この運賃を収得するために要する船員の給料、燃料代および揚げ切りまでの仕向け港の港費等の費用を控除
正味到達価額

(4) コンテナ

コンテナの正体価額
損害額を控除
共同海損に認容された損害額を加算
正味到達価額

(5) 貨　物

貨物のCIF価額
CIF価額ベースの損害額を控除
共同海損に認容されたCIF価額ベースの損害額を加算
正味到達価額

●貨物の共同海損負担額は、以下のように計算します。

【ケース1】貨物にPA損害（破損、火災による焼損等）がある場合

| | |
|---|---:|
| CIF価額 | US$10,000 |
| CIF価額ベースの損害額を控除 | (-) 1,000 |
| 貨物の共同海損負担価額 | US$9,000 |

【ケース2】貨物に犠牲損害（船火事の際の消火注水による損害等）がある場合

| | |
|---|---:|
| CIF価額 | US$10,000 |
| CIF価額ベースの損害額を控除 | (-) 500 |
| CIF価額ベースの犠牲損害の金額（共同海損認容額）を加算 | 500 |
| 貨物の共同海損負担価額 | US$10,000 |

【ケース3】貨物にPA損害（焼損）US $1,000と犠牲損害（船火事の際の消火注水による損害）US $500がある場合

| | |
|---|---|
| CIF価額 | US$10,000 |
| CIF価額ベースの損害額を控除 | (-) 1,500 |
| CIF価額ベースの犠牲損害の金額を加算 | 500 |
| 貨物の共同海損負担価額 | US$9,000 |

---ポイント---
　貨物の共同海損負担額は、CIF価額の110％等の保険金額ベースではなく、CIF価額ベースで計算します。

# 第3章

## 「サルサ♪ カリブの海賊」共同海損

### 1 サルサ♪とハバナ旧市街、そして、カリブの海賊

　皆さん、ラテン音楽のサルサ♪（スペイン語で食卓のソースのこと）を聴いたり、踊ったりしたことはありますか。サルサのリズムは、拍子木で、サ、サ、サ、サルサ♪、サ、サ、サ、サルサ♪、と打ちます。サルサ♪はニューヨークの中南米出身者の間でキューバのソンやいろいろな音楽が混ざって生まれた、とても楽しいペアダンスです。

　私はこのダンスに魅せられ、キューバで柔道のトップ選手だったキューバ人の先生に六本木で習い始めてからすでに20年以上経ちます。周りのラテン音楽好きの友人に刺激され、本場キューバの音楽やダンスをもっと知りたくなり、日本から見るとちょうど地球の反対側にあり、かなり遠いのですが、キューバに何度も音楽・ダンス関係者と出かけました。キューバの首都ハバナは、私のとても好きな街です。

　アメリカがキューバと国交正常化したことから、最近よくキューバの様子がテレビに映ります。ハバナ旧市街は世界遺産に登録されており、スペイン植民地時代の建物や要塞がそのまま残されています。

　ハバナ市紋章は鍵と要塞。ハバナ湾は天然の良港で、16世紀頃には新大陸のスペインの植民地からの多くの物資がいったんハバナに運ばれ、本国に向かう商船に積み替えられスペインまで運ばれました。

【ハバナ市紋章】

まさにハバナは新大陸からスペイン本国に通じるドアで、その鍵が紋章に描かれています。また、金銀財宝が集まるハバナや、富を満載してハバナから本国に向かうスペインの商船は、カリブの海賊に何度も襲われました。通商および軍事的な要衝であったハバナを守るためにスペインは多くの要塞を築いたので、この要塞も紋章の図柄として表れているわけです。

## 2　海賊と共同海損

　海賊と言えば、数年前までアフリカ東岸ソマリア沖海域で、海賊による商船乗っ取り事件が続発しましたが、この海域の海賊は日本の海上自衛隊も参加する多国籍の艦船による商船護衛が功を奏し、ようやく下火になりました。今は、西アフリカ沖やマラッカ・シンガポール海峡の海賊が問題になっています。
　現代の海賊は、船舶と貨物を解放する対価として金銭を要求してきます。日本の法律では、海賊に乗っ取られた船舶と貨物を取り戻すために、財産の所有者が海賊にお金を支払うことが合法か、違法か、ということは明確ではありません。しかし、皆さんは少し驚かれるかもしれませんが、イギリスの法律では、船舶と貨物を取り戻すために海賊に解放金を支払うことは違法ではなく、「解放金の支払いはさらなる海賊行為を誘発する可能性があるが、船舶、貨物、乗組員の保護という目的のための解放金支払いの必要はこれに優り、解放金支払いを公序良俗違反とするにたる明白かつ危急の理由はない。」とする判決[4]も下されています。したがって、船舶と貨物を海賊から取り戻すために要した費用は、船舶と貨物を海賊という共同の危険から救う費用として共同海損に認容する精算実務がイギリスでは定着していると言えます。
　ただし、海賊がテロリストでないことが条件です。テロリストに対して資金を提供することは、どの国でも違法とされ、そのような支出費用は共同海損には認容されません。

## 3　共同海損の基本原理

　第2章で、世界を航行する船舶やそれにより運ばれる貨物にかかわる共同海損の取扱いを定めた統一規則であるヨーク・アントワープ規則A条で、共同海損を次のように定義していることをご説明しました。
　「共同の航海団体を構成する財産を危険から守る意図をもって、共同の安全のため

---

[4] Masefield AG v Amlin Corporate Member Ltd 事件（"Bunga Melati Dua" 号事件）［2011］EWCA Civ 24 & ［2010］EWHC 280 (Comm)。

に、故意にかつ合理的に、異常な犠牲を払い、または費用を支出した場合に限り、共同海損行為が成立する。」

そして、「共同海損は、船舶と貨物を救うための費用や、損害、および航海を完遂するために必要な費用や損害を、航海終了時の価額に応じて、救われた財産で傾斜配分して『割り勘』する仕組み」と、ご理解ください、と述べました。そのうえで、共同海損負担価額、共同海損分担額という用語や数字を使って、共同海損の大まかな仕組みについてご説明しました。

皆さん、おぼろげに共同海損の仕組みが見えてきたと思いますので、この章では、その内容をもう少し掘り下げてみたいと思います。

まず、共同海損の基本原理です。実は上記 YAR A 条に、その基本原理が詰まっています。

### (1) 共同の航海団体を構成する財産

共同海損が成立するためには、まず、航海にかかわる2つ以上の（複数の）財産がなければなりません。通常、共同海損は、船舶と貨物という2つの財産で成立しますが、船舶に貨物が積まれていない場合でも、船舶が、船主（貸主）から用船者（借主）に貸し出され、用船者が所有する燃料がある場合には、船舶と用船者が所有する燃料の2つの財産があり、共同海損が成立します。

逆に、船舶が貨物を積載しておらず、用船者に貸し出されてもいない場合には、航海にかかわる財産は船舶だけ（1つ）ですから、共同海損は成立しません。

### (2) 共同の危険

共同海損が成立するためには、上記の2つ以上の財産に共同の危険が発生していなければなりません。共同の危険があったかどうかについては、事案ごとに判断するしかありませんが、危険が切迫したものであることを要しないものの、現実のものでなければなりません。逆に言えば、危険が発生する可能性があるだけでは要件を満たしません。

しかし、たとえば、たくさんの船舶が頻繁に通航する狭く潮流も速い航路（海峡等の狭水路）で、船舶のエンジンが故障し、漂流状態になった場合、今すぐ沈没する状態ではないものの、船舶をまったく操船することができなくなっているため、潮流に流されて、座礁したり、他の船舶と衝突したりする危険があり、船舶と貨物に共同の危険があるものと判断されます。

### (3) 故意かつ合理的な行為

共同海損になるためには、船舶と貨物等の航海にかかわる財産を救うために、故意

（意図的）かつ合理的な行為が必要とされます。これを共同海損行為と呼びます。

たとえば、船舶が座礁した際に、船主が船舶と貨物を救うために救助船を手配し、岩場からの曳き下ろし作業を依頼したとします。船舶が座礁したという偶然の出来事は、共同海損になりませんが[5]、船舶と貨物を救うために、船主が救助船を手配し、船舶を岩場から曳き下ろす行為は、故意かつ合理的な行為であり、この行為により生じた船舶や貨物に生じた損害は共同海損になります。

### (4) 異常な犠牲または費用

共同海損行為によって生じた損害または費用は、通常の航海で生じるものではなく、異常なものでなければなりません。逆に言えば、貨物を運送するために通常生じる船舶運航に関する費用等は共同海損にはなりません。

たとえば、海難事故が発生し、船舶と貨物の共同の安全のために、あえて最寄りの安全な港（避難港）に入り、避難港で修繕を行い、安全に当初の仕向け港までの航海を継続できる状態になり、仕向け港に向かう元の航路に船舶が復帰しました。この場合には、安全な港に向けて避難を開始した時から元の航路に復帰した時までに本船で通常消費される燃料代は共同海損費用に認容されません。しかし、避難入港という共同海損行為によって、通常航海消費量を超えて消費された余分な燃料代は、共同海損に認容されることとなります。

いかがでしょう、共同海損の基本原理、成立要件が、少し身近に感じられませんか。海難事故が発生すれば、すべて共同海損になるわけではなく、相当細かく厳格な要件があり、ルールの字句についても長い歴史がありますので、非常に多くの事例を積み重ねることによって、字句の意味が明確にされ、共同海損の形が相当具体的にできあがっていると言えます。そして、われわれ海損精算人は、共同海損に関するルールの内容、事例の積み重ね、海運、貿易、海上保険に関する法律、実務等を学んで、個々の事案が起きたときに、その知見に基づき、船主、荷主等の航海に関係する皆さんに、適宜必要有益な助言をしながら、共同海損の精算を行い、事案解決のお手伝いをしているのです。

### ④ 最後に、カリブの海賊からの贈り物、冷えたモヒートはいかが

冒頭でご紹介したハバナは、文豪アーネスト・ヘミングウェイがこよなく愛し、「老人と海」を書き上げた街としても有名です。フロリダ半島南端キーウエストの南

---

[5] 座礁による船体損傷修繕費は、船舶単独で負担すべき費用（単独海損費用）で、多くの船舶保険で修繕費として保険金支払いの対象になります。

方沖にあり、いつも暑いキューバでは、どうしても冷たい飲み物が欲しくなります。ヘミングウェイは「モヒート」（ラム酒をベースにライム、炭酸水、砂糖、ミントの葉を入れたカクテル）が大好きだったようです。モヒートは、16世紀後半、新大陸から得られる富をスペインと争っていたイギリス女王エリザベス1世の支援を受けた海賊フランシス・ドレークの部下が、キューバの人たちに伝えた、と言われています。

　これは猛暑の日本の夏でもお薦めです。まだ飲んだことのない人はぜひお試しください。ハバナの要塞やカリブの海賊や共同海損のことを思い浮かべながら、冷えたモヒートを楽しんでいただければと思います。

# 第4章

# 共同海損認容に関する2つの基本思想
（共同の安全と航海の完遂）

## 1  ニューヨークの自由の女神像

　もう20年以上前になりますが、海損精算実務を学ぶためにニューヨークに派遣された際、ダウンタウンのウォール街に近い研修先に9か月間通いました。とても多くのことを学びましたが、仕事以外の思い出もたくさんあります。ランチタイムには、よく若い海損精算人と一緒にピザかサンドイッチ、そしてコーラを買って、マンハッタン島最南端にあるバッテリーパークに向かいました。

　晴れて天気が良い日には、バッテリーパークから自由の女神像が見えます。私はこの眺めがとても気に入っていました。でも、自由の女神像を遠くからしか眺められないので、アメリカ人の友人と、時折マンハッタン島の沖合に浮かぶスタテン島との間を往復している地元の通勤客が利用するフェリーに乗り、スタテン島で降りないで、そのままバッテリーパークに戻って来ました。

【お返しとしてパリに住むアメリカ人たちがフランス革命百周年を記念して贈った
　パリ セーヌ河畔に立つ自由の女神像】

I わかりやすい共同海損

　こうすると、昼休みにピザやサンドイッチを食べながら、2つの島の間にある自由の女神像を近くでゆっくり2回見ることができるのです。
　皆さんご存知のとおり、ニューヨークの自由の女神像は、アメリカ合衆国独立百周年を記念してフランスから贈呈され1886年に完成しました。アメリカの自由のシンボルですが、この女神像はマンハッタン島の方には向いていません。自由の国アメリカを目指してはるばる大西洋を渡って来た移民たちを歓迎するかのように、大西洋に向かって立っているのです。
　この懐かしいニューヨークで、2016年5月3日から6日まで世界各国から法律家や実務家が出席し万国海法会[6]第42回国際会議が開催され、2016年ヨーク・アントワープ規則（YAR 2016）が採択されました。
　YAR 2016は、国際的な船主団体もその内容を支持しており、徐々に、現在最もよく利用されている1994年ヨーク・アントワープ規則（YAR 1994）からYAR 2016に切り替わって行くものと思います。YAR 1994との相違点については、第8章でご説明します。

## ② 共同海損認容に関する2つの基本思想

　第3章で、世界を航行する船舶やそれにより運ばれる貨物にかかわる共同海損の取扱いを定めた統一規則であるヨーク・アントワープ規則（YAR）A条に述べられた共同海損の基本原理について詳しくご説明しました。
　これから、もう一歩進んで、共同海損の2つの基本思想（考え方）についてご説明したいと思います。大まかに言ってYARに基づき共同海損に認められる損害や費用は、次の2つです。

(1)　**船舶と貨物が現実に危険に瀕している際に、船舶と貨物の共同の安全を確保するために生じた損害や費用**
　たとえば、船火事を消すためにカーゴホールド（貨物船の船内にある貨物が積まれる場所）に水を注入した結果、船舶や貨物に生じた損害や、救助報酬、座礁した船舶を浮揚させるために貨物の一部を艀（はしけ）に下ろす費用です。

---

[6]　万国海法会は、1897年に設立された海法の国際的統一を目的として設立された各国国内海法会を会員とする国際機関（ベルギーの公益法人で、会員海法会は現在約50）。

## 第4章 共同海損認容に関する2つの基本思想（共同の安全と航海の完遂）

(2) 当初予定していた航海を完遂するために、言い換えれば、船舶と貨物の共同の利益のために支出された費用[7]

これは、海難事故が発生し、船舶が避難のために最寄りの安全な港（避難港）に入港した後、船舶の海難損傷修繕費以外の当初の航海を安全に再開するために支出された費用です。たとえば、避難港で航海を完遂するために必要な修繕を施工するために必要とされた貨物の仮揚げ、保管および本船への再積込み費用や、避難港における船舶修繕期間中の本船船員の給料等、ならびに避難港から船舶が出港するために要した港費です。

上記の「共同の安全」と「航海の完遂」という2つの基本思想は、現在、整然と整理され、その差異にもかかわらず、互いに正当に共同海損に認容される損害や費用としてYARに規定されています。では、なぜ、この2つの基本思想が共存しているのでしょうか。共同海損の歴史から見るとよく理解できます。

共同海損について、伝統的にイギリスの法律では、船舶と貨物の共同の安全が確保された（船舶が避難港に入港し、安全が確保された）時点で共同海損が終了するとの考えを採用し、フランス等のヨーロッパ大陸諸国の法律では、当初予定していた航海が完了した時点で共同海損が終了するとの考えを採用していました。

航海を共にする船主と荷主の国籍が異なる場合、国によって共同海損についての考え方が異なると、共同海損に認容される金額が異なり、共同海損として精算することができません。

そこで、19世紀後半、多くの海事関係者が共同海損の規則を統一するためには、共同海損に関する統一法の制定が望ましいと考え、この目標に向かって長年努力しました。しかし、種々の利害関係が複雑に入り混じりなかなか目標を達成しにくいため、次に「共同海損規則の自主的統一」、すなわち、統一規則を作り、その規則を船主と荷主が運送契約に取り入れることに合意することによって、実質的な統一を達成することを目指したのです。

1860年にグラスゴー決議（Glasgow Resolutions 1860）、1864年にヨーク規則（York Rules）、1877年にヨーク・アントワープ規則（York-Antwerp Rules）が採択されました。ようやくYARが産声を上げたわけです。

このような関係者の長い間の努力の積み重ねによって、現在では、ほとんどすべての運送契約中にYARが取り入れられ合意されています。

---

(7) 船舶と貨物の共同の安全を確保するために生じた損害や費用は、YARの明文の規定によって除外されない限り共同海損になりますが、航海を完遂するために支出された費用は、YARの明文の規定で共同海損に認容される場合に限り、共同海損に認容されます。

## ③ 共同海損の成立時点

次に、共同海損はどの時点で成立するのかについて考えてみましょう。座礁、火災、衝突等の共同海損事故が発生し、船舶と貨物を救うための共同海損行為がなされた時点でしょうか。それとも仕向け港における航海終了（共同海損事故発生時に本船に積載されていた貨物の揚げ荷役終了）時点でしょうか。

答えは、仕向け港における航海終了の時点です。仕向け港に船舶と貨物が到着し、事故発生当時本船に積載されていた貨物の揚げ荷役が終了し、航海が終了した時点で、初めて共同海損を分担すべき財産の価額が確定し、共同海損が成立します。

海難事故の後、船舶が避難のために入った港（避難港）で、救助等の共同海損行為によっていったん船舶と貨物が救われていたとしても、船舶と貨物が仕向け港（目的港）に到着し、航海が終了しなければ、共同海損は成立しません。仕向け港で航海が終了して初めて共同海損を案分して分担する（支払う）財産（原資）が確定します。

したがって、避難港から仕向け港に向かう途中で、衝突等の別の事故により船舶と貨物が全損になってしまった場合は、共同海損行為はありましたが、航海終了時点で共同海損を分担する利益が残らなかったので、共同海損は成立しないのです。

割り勘を支払う原資が確定しなければ、共同海損は最終的に成立しない、とご理解ください。

## ④ 共同海損分担利益（共同海損行為の結果、救われた財産）

共同海損を分担する（割り勘を支払う）のはどのような財産でしょうか。

これまでの説明でご理解いただけると思います。すなわち、共同海損事故が発生した時点で、共同の危険にさらされていた船舶およびそれに積載されていた貨物、コンテナ、本船の燃料等のすべての財産が、共同海損行為によって航海終了時に救われていますので、その時点における救われたそれぞれの価額に応じて共同海損を分担します。

## ⑤ 共同海損負担価額（共同海損行為の結果、救われた財産の航海終了時における価額）

ここでの最後のテーマは、共同海損の割り振りの基準についてです。共同海損は、仕向け港（目的港）における船舶や貨物の救われた財産の正味到達価額に基づき、案分して負担（分担）されます。

船舶については、航海終了時（または貨物全量が仕向け港まで代船により輸送された

場合は、避難港における代船からの貨物揚げ切り時）の船舶の正体市場価額評価額から共同海損に認容されない修繕費を控除した金額が、共同海損負担額になります。船舶の市場価額は、世界経済状況により著しく変動します。船舶の売買を実際に仲介しているイギリスの船舶売買仲介業者兼船価鑑定人、または日本海運集会所等の鑑定人による評価額を、海損精算人が、船舶の正体市場価額として共同海損精算で採用します。

　貨物については YAR1994 第17条で、商業送り状価額（CIF価額）が航海終了時の貨物の価額と規定されているので、この価額から、航海終了までの共同海損に認容されない損害（偶然的な事故の結果生じた損害）額を控除した金額が、貨物の共同海損負担額になります。

　30数年前までは、本船の燃料（バンカーオイル）の価額が比較的安く、船舶の価額に含まれているものとみなして、独立した財産として考慮しなくても済みましたが、その後の燃料価額の上昇に伴い、現在、燃料は、船舶とは別の分担利益として共同海損を分担します。

## 6　最後にコーラで乾杯

　長年、自由の女神像の祝福を受け、船に乗って入ってくる移民を受け入れてきたニューヨークで、2016年ヨーク・アントワープ規則が採択されたことを海損精算人の1人として嬉しく思っています。

　今回はモヒートではなく、ニューヨークに思いをはせ、コーラで乾杯したいと思います。

# 第5章

# どんな費用が共同海損に認められるのでしょうか

## 1 イギリス人の生涯の師

イギリスは何かにつけて話題の多い国ですが、海に囲まれたこの国にはロイズを始めとする世界有数の海上保険市場があり、優秀な海事弁護士や、海損精算人が多数います。いったん海難事故が起きると、われわれ日本の海損精算人も、船舶や貨物といったすべての航海関係者にとって有益な場合には、イギリスの海損精算人と日英連名で共同海損精算書を発行（ジョイント・アジャストメント）することもあります。

このような背景から、イギリスの海損精算人と気軽に話せる個人的なつながりを維持することは、日本の海損精算人にとってきわめて重要です。もうずいぶん昔になりますが、私は、海損精算実務の修得とイギリス海損精算人との人脈形成を目的として、1991年6月中旬から3か月間、英国に派遣されロンドンの金融街シティにある研修先に通いました。

研修期間中に、ロイズを訪問したことも忘れられない思い出になっています。実際に保険取引が行われているアンダーライング・ルームや、現在は特別な場合に限って鳴らされるルーティーン・ベル[8]を見学しました。大学時代、一橋大学の木村栄一先生が書かれた『ロイズ——世界最大の保険市場』[9]を読んで、とても気になっていた海上保険の歴史と伝統を体感できる特異な「場」の雰囲気（アトモスフィア）を体験することができました。保険関係者の皆さん、機会があれば、ぜひ訪ねてみてはいかがでしょうか。

研修先では、数多くの優秀な海損精算人を育成した教育者でもある Jim O'Shea が私のメンターとして付き、毎日厳しくかつ温かく指導してくれました。彼は、海損精算について教えるだけでなく、海運、海上貿易のルールを覚え、またロイズリスト等

---

(8) アンダーライング・ルームの中央に吊るされている古びた鐘。タイタニック号沈没等の悲報には1回、アポロ11号無事帰還等の吉報には複数回鳴らされます。もともとは、1799年金銀地金等100万ポンドを超える財宝を積載し航行中、オランダ沖で座洲した英国海軍フリゲート艦「ルーティーン号」に付いていた鐘。

(9) 木村栄一『ロイズ——世界最大の保険市場』（日経新書、1981）。

の海事新聞や一般の新聞をよく読んで、広く一般社会の常識を身につけることの大切さを説いていました。3か月間の研修の後も、彼がいるロンドンの事務所を訪問したり、電話、メール等で個別事案について相談し、私には生涯の師とも言うべき存在になりました。

　研修から約20年後の2012年5月に、ロンドンで事務弁護士をしているご子息のJohnからJimの訃報が届きました。JohnはJimがずっと私のことを気にかけていたので、私に訃報を知らせようと思ったものの、私の連絡先がわからないので、研修中にJimと私の2人で撮った写真を持って、わざわざ私の知り合いがいるロンドンの事務所を訪問し私に知らせるよう頼んでくれたそうです。JimとJohnの思いに触れてとても胸が熱くなりました。

## 2　イギリス人は割り勘が嫌い？

　滞在していた頃を思い出すと、ロンドンの地下鉄のホームではいつも「マインド・ザ・ギャップ、プリーズ」（Mind the gap, please. ホームと電車の間の溝（ギャップ）に注意してください）、というアナウンスが流れていました。アメリカのように「Watch your step」と言わず、イギリスでは「mind」を使います。この表現はとても奥が深く「自分と他者との認識の違い（ギャップ）に心配りしなさい」と教えてくれているような気がしました。海損精算人にとって、船主さんと荷主さんのどちらにも偏らず両方の視点から見て、衡平な共同海損の精算を心がけなさい、と言っているように私には聞こえました。

　ロンドンは多くの皆さんが思われているより緯度が高く、北海道の北にあるサハリンの中央くらいにあります。しかし、そのお陰で、夏は夜9時過ぎまで明るく湿度も低いのでとても快適でした。

　アフターファイブには、研修先の皆さんと何度かパブに出かけ、オフィスだけでは得られない貴重な生の情報が聴けました。独特な形のパイントグラス（568ミリリットルのビアグラス）で飲む現地のビールはけっこうおいしいのですが、イギリス人は日本人のようにおつまみを取らないで、立ったままなめるように時間をかけて飲みながらいろいろな話をします。日本でビールをゴクゴク飲むことに慣れていた私には、現地の飲み方に慣れるのに、少し時間がかかりました。

　もう1つ驚いたことには、日英の文化の違いでしょうか、イギリスのパブで友達と一緒に飲みに行った際に、一人ひとり別々に飲み物を買う、または、後で割り勘にするのはマナー違反のようです。たとえば5人でパブに行くと、別々に注文したり、割り勘にしたりしないで、1杯目はAさん「僕がおごるよ。みんな何がいい？」（It's my round. What are you having?）と言って、5人全員のビール代を払い（おごり）、次にB

さんが「今度は私の番」と言って全員のビール代を払い、その次はCさんが全員のビール代を支払います。何杯も飲めば、いちいち割り勘しなくても、だんだん衡平な分担になり、とても賢いやり方だと思いました。

## 3 どんな費用が共同海損になるのでしょうか？

さて、共同海損に話を戻しましょう。共同海損になるためには、①船舶と貨物が共同の危険から脱する（救われる）ことに加えて、②船舶と貨物が仕向け港に到着し、航海が完了することが必要です。

それでは、どのような費用が共同海損の枠組みで認められるのでしょうか。

### (1) 共同海損の基本形

海上運送人は、運送契約上、運賃を収得する代わりに貨物を無事に仕向け港まで運送する義務を負っていますので、船主は、共同海損になるような大事故が発生した場合には、まず自力で、もしくは手配した救助船に曳航され、本船を避難港に入港させ、安全を確保したうえで、航海継続のために必要とされる検査や修繕を行い、本船で貨物を仕向け港まで運送することを考えます。これが、共同海損の基本形です。

この基本形に沿って対処すれば、航海完遂のために余分に要した費用の大半は、ヨーク・アントワープ規則に基づき共同海損に認容されます。すなわち本船で仕向け港まで運送する場合には、通常以下の費用が、共同海損に認容されます。

① 救助報酬（救助業者に支払われる報酬）
② 本船の避難港への入出港に伴う港費および代理店費用（ただし、もっぱら修繕に関するものは除きます）
③ 仕向け港までの航海を安全に完遂するために必要な本船の損傷修繕を施工するために貨物を仮揚げする必要がある場合には、貨物の仮揚げ、保管および修繕完了後、仮揚げした貨物の本船への再積込み費用
④ 本船の避難入港に伴う離路期間[10]中の本船船員の給料手当、食料金、ならびにその間に消費された本船の燃料、清水代

---

[10] ここでいう離路期間とは、本船事故発生後、避難港に向けて避難（移動）を開始した時から避難港入港後、原航路に復帰するまでに実際に要した時間から、事故が発生しなかったとすれば、事故発生地点から原航路復帰地点までの通常航海に要したであろう所要見込み時間を控除した期間（つまり事故が起こらなかった場合よりも余分にかかった時間）のことです。頻繁に共同海損に認容される費用で、精算書によく出てきますが、言葉だけでは、わかりにくいので、図表2をご覧ください。

**図表2** 本船の避難入港に伴う離路期間

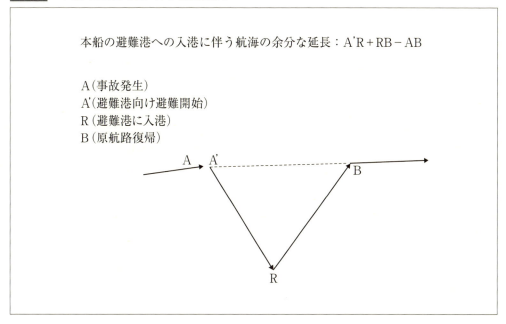

## (2) 早期に貨物を仕向け港まで運送するための代替手段（基本形を限度に共同海損に認容）

しかし、この基本形どおりに話が進む場合ばかりではありません。実際には、いろいろな事情によって、この基本形から離れた手順で事態が進む場合がよくあります。

たとえば、避難港における本修繕が長期間になることが見込まれる場合に、早期に貨物を仕向け港まで運送するための代替手段（オプション）として、以下の方法が考えられ、実行されます。

① 仮修繕を施工して、貨物を積載した本船が仕向け港まで続航する。
② 貨物全量を代船に積み替えて、仕向け港まで継送する。
③ 避難港から、そのまま仕向け港まで本船を曳航する。

これらの代替手段をとった結果、余分に要した(i)仮修繕費、(ii)代船輸送費用、または(iii)仕向け港までの曳航費用は、避難港、または避難港で本修繕が施工できない場合は最寄りの本修繕が可能な港で本修繕を施工した場合に、共同海損に認められたであろう貨物の仮揚げ、保管および仮揚げした貨物の本船への再積み費用の見込み額（「共同海損の基本形」をとった場合の共同海損認容見込み額）を限度に、「代換費用」（代わりに要した費用）として、共同海損に認められます。

つまり、代替手段をとることによって余分にかかった費用を、先に述べた基本形のとおり進んだとすれば発生し共同海損に認められたであろう費用を限度に、共同海損に認めようというものです。なお、余分にかかった代船輸送費用や曳航費用からは、

事故が起こらなかったとすれば通常の航海のために要したであろう費用は節約されたものとして差し引かれます。

## ④ 最後は、アフタヌーンティの優雅なひとときを

　イギリスと言えば、やはりアフタヌーンティですね。1840年頃、第7代ベッドフォード公爵フランシス・ラッセルの夫人、アンナ・マリアが、午後9時過ぎまでパーティやオペラ鑑賞といった夜の社交があって、どうしても夕食が遅くなってしまうので、お茶の時間に軽食をとるようになり、アフタヌーンティが生まれた、と言われています。たまには、日本でもイギリスにいる気分で、家族や友人と紅茶を飲み、おしゃべりしながら、サンドイッチや、スコーン、デザートを楽しむ時間を持つのもいいかもしれません。

　私はイギリス滞在中、ローマ風呂の遺跡で有名なイングランド南西部のバース（Bath、そうです。お風呂という英語単語の起源と言われる街です）を観光し、クラシック音楽の弦楽4重奏を聴きながら、ゆったり、まったりした気分で、楽しんだアフタヌーンティが忘れられません。ちなみに、もうローマ風呂に入ることはできませんが、健康に良い温泉水を飲むことができます。

# 第6章

# どんな損害が共同海損に認められるのでしょうか

## 1 冬の星座——オリオンのギリシャ神話

　趣味としては、サルサを踊るのが一番楽しくて好きですが、その次はと言うと、高校で地学部に所属していた頃から星を観ることが大好きです。地学部の同級生で、趣味の天体観測の道を進み国立天文台に勤務している友人や、天文雑誌に天体写真を投稿している先輩もいます。高校、大学時代よく地学部の仲間と、蓼科、奥只見、野辺山等に出かけ、寝袋に入り肉眼や天体望遠鏡を使って天体を観測し、天体写真を撮りました。蓼科では、今にも空から落ちてきそうな天の川を見て感動しました。どんなに忙しくても夜空を眺める心のゆとりを持ち続けたいものです。

　とくに冬は空がよく澄みオリオン座が美しい季節です。ギリシャ神話で、海の神ポセイドンの子で、狩りの名手オリオンは、この世に自分が倒せない獲物はいない、とおごっていたため、さそりの毒針に刺され命を落としてしまい、さそりと共に天に上げられ星座になってしまいました。オリオンは冬の間、空の高いところで威張っていますが、明け方、さそりが東の空から昇ると西の空に沈んでしまいます。自信過剰は災難の元ですね。気を付けましょう。

【「星座書ウラノメトリア」に描かれたオリオン座】

出典：『星座書ウラノメトリア』（アメリカ海軍天文台所蔵、1603）

帆船時代は、夜空の星々を眺めての天文航法であり、海と空（星）はつながっていました。今では人工衛星を使ったGPSが利用され、新しい形で海と空（衛星）がつながり、大洋を航行する船舶の運航もより安全になっています。しかし、どんなに気を付けていても、船舶機器の故障や、船員の過失（ヒューマンエラー）等により、残念ながら座礁、衝突等の海難事故は起きてしまいます。このような背景から、損害や費用を案分して分担する共同海損の仕組みが3,000年近く続いているわけですが。ともかく、このように昔から海と星の関係は深く、星に姿を変えたギリシャ神話の登場人物の名前が、今でも多くの船に付けられています。

## ② どんな損害が共同海損になるのでしょうか？

　第5章で、船舶と貨物を共同の危険から救うための費用や、仕向け港までの航海を完遂するために支出された余分な費用が共同海損に認容されることをご説明しました。しかし、支出された費用だけではなく、船舶と貨物を救うためにあえて（故意に）行った共同海損行為の結果、船舶や貨物に生じた損害も同様に共同海損に認容されます。

　それでは、どんな損害が共同海損になるのか、具体的に見ていきましょう。

### (1) 火災の際、消火作業によって船舶や貨物に生じた損害

　火災は、船舶と貨物を共同の危険にさらす代表的な事故です。火災が発生した場合、火災により直接、船舶や貨物に損害（焼損、煙または熱による損害）が生じ、消火作業としてカーゴホールド（船内の貨物を保管する場所）等に注水することによって船舶や貨物に損害が生じることがあります。

　火災によって直接被った損害は、火災という偶発的な（偶然起こった）事故によって船舶や貨物が被る損害なので、船舶や貨物が単独で負担します。単独で負担する損害という意味から、単独海損損害（Particular Average）またはPA損害と呼ばれます。

　他方、消火作業の結果、船舶や貨物に生じた水濡れ損害や錆び損害は、船舶と貨物を救うためにあえて行った共同海損行為の結果生じた損害ですので、犠牲損害として共同海損に認容されます。共同海損犠牲損害と呼ばれます。

### (2) 救助作業の結果、船舶や貨物に生じた損害

　船舶と貨物を共同の危険から救う救助行為の結果、船舶や貨物に生じた損害も同様に、犠牲損害として共同海損に認容されます。

　具体例を以下にご紹介します。

　たとえば、座礁した船舶を離礁させるために貨物の一部をバージ（はしけ）に瀬取

り（仮揚げ）、離礁後、仮揚げした貨物を本船に再積込みした場合、この貨物の瀬取り、再積込み作業によって船舶や貨物に生じた損害は共同海損に認容されます。

　また、座礁した船舶を離礁させるために貨物が投棄（投荷）された場合には、この貨物の損害は、共同海損犠牲損害になります。ただし、近年、危険物や有害物質の海洋投棄は法律により禁止されており、実際に投荷が行われることはあまりありません。

　さらに座礁によって生じた船体の損傷は船舶の単独海損になりますが、救助行為として、たとえば、救助船等による曳き下ろし作業によって生じた船体損傷、および乗り揚げて危険な状態にある船舶を離礁させるためにエンジンを強行使用した結果エンジンに生じた損害は、共同海損犠牲損害になります。

### (3) 避難港における荷役に伴う船舶や貨物の損害

　航海を完遂するために必要とされる本船の本修繕を施工するための貨物の仮揚げ、再積込み作業や、代船への積替え作業に伴う船舶や貨物の損害も、共同海損犠牲損害として認容されます。

　とくに原油、ケミカル製品、穀物等のばら積み貨物では、荷役を繰り返すと、どうしても欠減損害（shortage）の数量が増加します（貨物の量が少なくなります）。事故がなかった場合の通常航海における通常の貨物の欠減量を超える余分な欠減損害が、共同海損犠牲損害として認容されます。

### (4) 共同の安全を確保するための荷直し作業によって生じた船舶や貨物の損害

　これからお話しするのは、私が共同海損精算人として共同海損鑑定人と共に救助作業現場に出張した記憶に残る事案です。

　鋼板のコイルを積載した貨物船が、日本から東南アジアに向けて航行中、東シナ海で荒天に遭遇し貨物が荷崩れを起こし、船体が最大40度近く傾斜し、転覆、沈没しかねない危険な状態になりました。このため、船員全員が本船から退避し、本船は無人の状態で漂流し続け、付近の浅瀬に座礁する危険がありました。

　船主は救助業者に救助を依頼し、本船は救助船に曳航され、船体傾斜したままの非常に不安定な状態ではありますが、なんとか最寄りの安全な港の那覇に避難入港することができました。しかし、多くの場合、船舶は避難港に入港すると、その港に留まる限りは、物理的に安全な状態になりますが、本件では避難港に入港しても、なお20数度船体が傾斜したままで、転覆、沈没する危険があり、船体が安定性を回復するまで、救助作業を続行することになりました。

　船主、船舶保険者からの要請もあり、共同海損鑑定人と共に共同海損精算人の私も、着岸し救助作業中の本船に乗船し、救助の指揮を執るサルベージマスターから状

況の説明を受けましたが、20度の船体傾斜は本当にきつく、危険を肌で感じました。

結果として、船体傾斜を直すために、本船は着岸し、陸上クレーンを使用することを決定し、積載された貨物を、本船が安定性を回復するまで、ヤードに仮揚げ、保管することにしました。

このように、共同の安全を確保するために貨物を仮揚げ、荷直しした場合、この貨物の仮揚げ、荷直し、横持ちおよび本船への再積込み作業中に、同作業によって船体と貨物に生じた損害は、共同海損に認容されます[11]。

### ③ 最後に、簡単な頭の体操をしましょう

最後に、共同海損として認められた損害（共同海損犠牲損害認容額）も、共同海損を分担することによって、船舶や貨物といった航海関係者間の衡平な分担を実現することができます。次の設例をよく読んでいただければ、共同海損3,000年の歴史に耐えた1つの真理をご理解いただけるものと思います。

**設 例** 共同海損犠牲損害認容額も共同海損を分担することによって衡平になる

貨物Bが消火注水作業によって濡れ損を被り全損になった場合、貨物Bが共同海損を分担しないですむとすれば、貨物Bは共同海損犠牲損害認容額の全額を他の分担利益から補償してもらい、他の分担利益と比べて優位になります。

| | 共同海損分担利益 | 共同海損負担価額 | 共同海損分担額 |
|---|---|---|---|
| 船　舶 | 正味到達価額100 | 100 | 34 |
| 貨物 A | CIF価額100 | 100 | 33 |
| **貨物 B** | CIF価額**100** | 0 | 0 |
| 貨物 C | CIF価額100 | 100 | 33 |
| | 合　　計 400 | 300 | 100 |

共同海損分担率：33.3％

そこで、消火注水作業により濡れ損を被り全損になった貨物Bも、あたかも救われたものとして共同海損を分担することにより、消火作業によって救われた他の分担利益と同様な立場になり、関係者間のバランスを保つことができます。

---

[11] 荷直しの費用が、単に航海中の荷崩れに起因する再積付けのために支出された場合は、その再積付けが共同の安全のために必要でない限り、共同海損に認容されません。荷直しが共同海損に認められない場合は、この荷直し作業によって船舶や貨物に生じた損害も共同海損犠牲損害として認容されないことに留意してください。

第6章　どんな損害が共同海損に認められるのでしょうか

|  | 共同海損分担利益 | 共同海損負担価額 | 共同海損分担額 |
|---|---|---|---|
| 船　　舶 | 正味到達価額 100 | 100 | 25 |
| 貨 物 A | CIF 価額 100 | 100 | 25 |
| **貨 物 B** | **CIF 価額 100** | **100** | **25** |
| 貨 物 C | CIF 価額 100 | 100 | 25 |
|  | 合　　計 <u>400</u> | 400 | 100 |

共同海損分担率：25.0％

# 第7章

## 船主の共同海損宣言
（貨物に共同海損の分担を求める手続き）

### 1　伝統の襷（たすき）をつなぐ駅伝の魅力

　皆さん、年末年始はゆっくり休んで、英気を養われましたか。お正月休みに、こたつでお餅を食べながら、テレビで箱根駅伝を楽しまれた方もいらっしゃるかもしれません。箱根駅伝は、東京大手町と箱根芦ノ湖との間を2日間かけて、往路5人、復路5人の大学生の選手が、母校の襷をつないで、途中、山頂に雪を抱く富士山を仰ぎ見ながら、新春の湘南海岸や、湯煙の箱根路を走り抜けます。

　私たちは一人ひとり、家庭での子育てや職場での後継者の育成等を通じて、誰もが、未来を担う次世代を育てています。毎日の生活の中で、山あり谷あり、苦しいことや悩みがある中で、自分が受け継いだ襷を、しっかり次世代に引継ごうと奮闘しているわけであり、そのような中で、多くの人が駅伝競技に共感し、ずっと人気が衰えないのかもしれませんね。

### 2　襷をつないだ大先輩と共同海損のバイブル

　襷をつなぐと言えば、忘れられない人がいます。私が、1983年に東京海損精算事務所に入社した際の社長、故宮武和雄氏です。小説『海賊とよばれた男』[12]に保険会社の保険金支払責任者として、実名で登場している人です。私が新入社員の頃、すでに70歳を超えていましたが、月曜から金曜の毎朝8時半から10時まで、海上保険の営業、業務、損害部門の若い人たちを対象に、海上保険や共同海損の英語で書かれた名著の輪読会を主宰していました。私も、海外研修に出るまで、7年間毎朝早朝勉強会に参加しました。海上保険の原理原則を懇切丁寧に語るだけでなく、長い海外経験で培われた英単語の発音やイントネーションの大切さも丁寧に教えていただきました。

　この大先輩がこの輪読会でテキストとして使用していた原書の1冊に、共同海損の

---

[12]　百田尚樹『海賊とよばれた男（上・下）』（講談社、2012・2014）。

バイブル（権威のある必読書）がありました。LowndesおよびRudolf共著『共同海損法およびヨーク・アントワープ規則〔第10版〕』（1975年発行）です。この本は、世界中の共同海損精算人が手元に置いて、いつも参照している書籍であり、私も輪読会の後も30年以上にわたって、お世話になっています。

　この本は、1873年初版発行のRichard Lowndes著『イングランドおよび諸外国の共同海損法』と、1926年初版発行のGeorge Rupert Rudolf著『ヨーク・アントワープ規則　その歴史と発展、1924年同規則に関する注釈』という2冊の本が、1948年にLowndesおよびRudolfとして1冊の本にまとめられたものです。

　その後、数名の編者によって、共同海損のその後の発展や進化、新しい判例などが取り入れられ、最新版は2018年に発行された第15版で、イギリスの海事法の関係者によって、しっかりと襷がつながっているバイブルと言えます。

### ③　船主の共同海損宣言

　さて、本題の共同海損に戻りましょう。これまで、共同海損に認められる費用や損害について、ご説明してきました。共同海損の仕組みは、荷口（関係する荷主の数）が比較的少ない原油タンカーや、鉄鉱石や石炭を輸送するばら積み貨物船にも、1万を超える荷口のコンテナ船にも等しく適用されます。

　貨物を積載した本船が航海中、大事故（衝突、座礁、火災、機関故障、荒天遭遇による荷崩れ船体傾斜など）に遭遇し、相当な金額が共同海損として見込まれる場合には、まず、船主は、共同海損精算人を選任し、荷主に対して共同海損を宣言することになります。

　通常、共同海損の宣言は、船舶と貨物が共同の危険から脱し、最寄りの安全な港に避難入港した（いったん船舶と貨物が救われた）直後に、船主が行います。

　この共同海損宣言は、船主が、本船に乗船していない荷主に対して、共同海損になる事態が起きたことを知らせると共に、共同海損になる費用と損害について、後日分担請求を行いますから準備をお願いします、と通知するものです。

　船主は、共同海損の宣言と共に、荷主に対して次のような要請をします。

① 　共同海損の宣言を受け、後日共同海損の分担に応じることを約束してください。

② 　それに加えて、共同海損精算書[13]ができあがったら、確実に支払うことを保証

---

[13] 共同海損精算書は、航海関係者によって支出された諸費用のうち、共同海損としていくら認められ、船舶と貨物といった分担利益が、それぞれいくら共同海損の分担額を支払うべきかを示した書面。多くの場合、専門知識を有する共同海損精算人が、船主の委嘱を受けて作成します。

してください。

③　共同海損の精算に使う貨物の価額を申告してください。

そして、船主は、荷主が船主もしくは共同海損精算人に、必要書類（上記のとおり、後日精算書が届いたら、きちんと支払います、と約束する書類。General Average Securities と呼ばれます）を提出しないと、仕向け港で受け荷主に貨物を引き渡さない旨、伝えてきます。しかし、なぜ船主が、このように貨物の引渡しを拒むことが、できるのでしょうか。

## ④　貨物から後日の支払いを約束してもらうためのよりどころ——マリタイム・リーエン

古代ギリシャやローマ時代、通信手段が未発達だったこともあり、船主と一緒に、荷主または荷主の代理人も交易船に上乗り（うわのり）として乗船していました。荒天に遭遇し、転覆、沈没の危険が生じたため、船舶と貨物を救うために、貨物の一部を荷主の了解を得て船外に投棄し、無事危難から脱し、仕向け港に到着することができました。

そして、この当時は、船長が仕向け港に無事到着し、航海が終了した時に、その船舶に上乗りしていた貨物関係者に対して、共同海損の分担額の支払いを求め、共同海損の精算と決済が終了していました。これは、共同海損の原始的な形で、関係者間の衡平を実現するための必要性から生まれた仕組みで、当時は、迅速、確実な精算方法でした。

しかし、現在では、皆さんお気付きのとおり、船舶が大型化し、多数、大量の貨物が頻繁に遠隔地に輸送され、非常に多くの関係者が関与し、貨物関係者が船舶に乗船していることはありません。船舶が救助されて避難港に入るだけでも、高額な費用がかかりますので、最終的に、船舶や貨物がそれぞれいくら共同海損として分担すればよいか、を算定する共同海損の精算に、ある程度の歳月を要するのが普通です。

そうなると、救助費や避難港入港費用などの多くの出費を余儀なくされた船主は、仕向け港で受け荷主に貨物を引き渡してしまうと、共同海損の精算が完了して貨物から共同海損の分担金を受け取るまで、その請求を行うための強制力を持たず、非常に弱い立場に置かれることになります。

そこで、たいていどこの国の法律でも、航海関係者が負担した共同海損費用や損害に関して、船主が仕向け港で、貨物から共同海損の支払いに対する保証を受け取るまでは、貨物にマリタイム・リーエン（留置権）を行使して、貨物をその管理下に置いて、荷主への引渡しを拒むことが認められています。

このマリタイム・リーエンというよりどころがあるおかげで、船主は荷主から「共

同海損精算書が届いたら、後日きちんとお支払いします」という約束を得ることができるのです。このような仕組みになっているので、船主は、各受け荷主に対して「共同海損の宣言をする際に、貨物の分担額を後日支払います」という約束の証を、仕向け港で船主またはその代理人に渡してください。そうしないと、船主として、貨物を引き渡すことはできません、と伝えてくるわけです。

「後日支払いの約束の証」として、船主から要求される共同海損分担に関する保証は、具体的には、以下の2つです。
① 受け荷主が署名した共同海損盟約書[14]
② 信頼できる貨物保険者が署名した分担保証状[15]。または、貨物が無保険や、貨物保険者の信用が低い場合には、貨物のCIF価額に、共同海損精算人が見込んだ共同海損分担率を乗じた現金供託金[16]（たとえば、CIF価額の20％など）

## 5 貨物保険と共同海損の関係

共同海損事故の際、貨物保険がとても役に立ちます。

貨物保険では、偶発的な事故によって生じた貨物自体の物的損傷（滅失または損傷）に加えて、通常、共同海損や、救助報酬の貨物分担額等の費用損害も、保険金支払いの対象になります。この貨物保険の機能をよりどころとして、船主および共同海損精算人は、保険会社が署名した分担保証状の提出を求めてくるのです。

日本の損害保険会社の信用度は海外でも高いので、どの船主、どの共同海損精算人も、日本の貨物保険会社が署名した分担保証状を信頼のおける担保として受け入れますが、保険会社の信用度が低い場合には、分担保証状の受入れを拒否され、信用度が高い銀行が発行する銀行保証状や、船主または共同海損精算人への現金供託金を要求されることがあります。事故が起きた時には、ご加入された貨物保険会社の信用度が問題になりますので、注意が必要です。

受け荷主、貨物保険者が、上述した共同海損分担保証関連書類を、船主または共同海損精算人に提出すれば、受け荷主は貨物を仕向け港で受け取ることができます。こ

---

[14] 受け荷主が、共同海損精算完了時に、共同海損の貨物分担額を船主に支払うことを保証する書面で、受け荷主による署名が必要とされます。英語でAverage Bondと呼ばれます。
[15] 貨物保険者が、共同海損精算完了時に、共同海損の貨物分担額を船主に支払うことを保証する書面で、貨物保険者による署名が必要とされます。英語でAverage Guaranteeと呼ばれます。
[16] 貨物保険に入っていない場合（すなわち、貨物が無保険の場合）、共同海損貨物分担額支払いの保証として、現金供託金を船主または共同海損精算人に支払うことが必要になります。仕向け港で自分の貨物を受け取るために、貨物の輸入代金に加えて、さらに現金を用立てることが必要になり大変です。

I わかりやすい共同海損

れで共同海損に関する受け荷主の皆さんの対応は完了します。

その後の共同海損分担額の支払いまでの共同海損精算人への対応は、受け荷主に代わり、すべて貨物保険会社が行います。

---

**ポイント**

◆共同海損事故発生当初の対応のポイント◆

① 船主は、船舶保険者・共同海損精算人に相談のうえ、船舶と貨物が、安全な港で、いったん救われたら、共同海損を宣言する。
② 荷主は、船主からの共同海損宣言状を受け取ったら、すぐに貨物保険者に連絡し、共同海損分担保証関連書類を、船主または共同海損精算人に提出し、仕向け港で貨物を受け取る。

---

## 6 襷をつなぐための新年の抱負

現在、日本人男性の平均寿命は80歳、健康寿命（日常的、継続的に、医療や介護に依存しないで生活できる期間）は71歳だそうです。若い時は、あまり健康に気を付けなくても、多くの人が健康に生活できるのですが、40歳を過ぎると、多くの人が仕事や不健康な食生活等により、健康のバランスを崩してしまい、健康維持のために、いろいろと積極的に努力することが必要になります。私も連日の暴飲暴食のため、40歳の頃、定期健康診断で医師から各種数値の悪化を指摘されました。まず、ウォーキングで減量し、週に2回以上、スポーツクラブに行き、運動するようになり、現在も続けています。

私は現在55歳ですが、4歳になる息子がいます。身長が1メートルを超え、好奇心旺盛な男の子です。11月15日に、健やかな成長を祈願するため、赤い羽織に袴姿の息子を連れて、家族で、実家の近くにある亀戸天神で七五三のお参りをし、心新たな気持ちになりました。写真館で家族写真を撮り、境内の菊の花や、亀池、東京スカイツリーが間近に見える太鼓橋を散策し、息子もとても喜んでいました。

この正月の私の誓いは、自分自身の健康に十分気を付けながら、息子が一人立ちできるまで、しっかり育て、仕事では、周囲の若い人たちにしっかりと共同海損に関する考え方を引き継いで、皆さんと同様、確実に次世代への襷を渡す努力を続けていきたい、というものです。

---

**トピックス2　共同海損の精算地**

通常船荷証券（B／L）等の運送契約には、共同海損の精算準則と精算地についての規定があります。よくある例は、「共同海損は、1994年ヨーク・アントワープ規則に準拠

し、運送人の選択する地で精算される」というものです。
　運送契約上の共同海損精算地がロンドンやニューヨークになっていても、日本の船主であれば、日本で共同海損の精算をした方が、関係者にとって便利なので、貨物関係者の承諾を得て、東京で共同海損の精算をすることもあります。

### トピックス3　GAサーベイの手配

　避難港において荷役作業（本船の損傷修繕を施工するための貨物の仮揚げ、保管および再積込み作業や、代船への積替え作業等）が必要な場合には、船主、船舶保険者または海損精算人が、GAサーベイを手配します。
　共同海損犠牲損害として認容される消火注水損害や、避難港での荷役作業がない場合には、原則GAサーベイは不要です。
　消火注水損害の認定、避難港での荷役作業の際に生じた貨物の損害の確認や、荷役費用を妥当な金額にするようなアドバイスがGAサーベイヤーの主たる責務です。
　GAサーベイは、共同海損の精算を行ううえでの補助的な資料ですので、通常の船舶や貨物の損傷検査と同様に、GAサーベイヤーとしてよく事実を調査していれば十分です。費用や損害が共同海損になるかどうかを判断するのは海損精算人です。
　典型的な代換費用として、正味代船輸送費用がありますが、通常避難港で本修繕を施工した場合に要したであろう貨物の保管料等の見込み額を限度に、正味代船輸送費用は、代換費用として、共同海損に認容されます。したがって、GAサーベイレポートに、この保管料等の見込み額を記載してもらいます。

### トピックス4　共同海損費用保険の付保

　予定していた航海が完了して初めて、船舶や貨物といった分担利益が、共同海損行為により助かったと言えます。したがって、航海完了時に共同海損の分担義務が生じます。
　避難港出港後、仕向け港に到着するまでに、別の事故により本船が沈没全損になった場合には、船主は支出済みの共同海損費用を、船舶保険者からも、貨物からも回収することができなくなってしまいます。
　このようなリスクをヘッジするために、船主は本船が避難港を出港するまでに、船舶保険者に共同海損費用保険（Average Disbursements Insurance）を申し込みます。
　共同海損費用保険の引受条件には、カバーの広いAverage Disbursements Clauses (A)と、ややカバーの狭いAverage Disbursements Clauses (B)がありますが、どちらの条件でもよいでしょう※。

　　※Average Disbursements Clauses (A)では、避難港出港後、別の事故により、少しでも共同海損の負担額が減少すれば、保険金が支払われますが、Average Disbursements Clauses (B)では、避難港出港後、別の事故により、共同海損の負担額が共同海損認容額を下回った場合にだけ、保険金が支払われます。

Ⅰ　わかりやすい共同海損

# 第8章

## ヨーク・アントワープ規則
### (海上運送契約で合意された共同海損精算のよりどころ)

### 1　コンテナ2万個積み超大型コンテナ船の登場

　私事で恐縮ですが、私の4歳の息子は、電車や車が大好きです。一緒に散歩していると、アメリカ製のタイヤがものすごく太い超大型ピックアップトラックを見かけました。子どもが「パパ、(ディズニー映画)カーズのモンスタートラック」と叫ぶので、「そうだね。あの車は、たくさんの自動車を運ぶ大きな船に載って、アメリカから日本まで運ばれて来たんだよ。まるで大きなビルのような船なんだ」と答えました。私が海や船の話をよくするので、息子は私が船を救う仕事をしていると思っているようです。

　日本は世界第3位の経済大国ですが、残念ながら資源に乏しく、四方を海に囲まれた島国のため、日々の活動を大きく海上輸送に依存しています。なんと、食糧、衣料、工業品の原材料から完成品まで、輸出入貨物の99％以上が、船で運ばれているのです。船が日本に住んでいる私たちの生活を支えている状況は、昔から変わらず、今後も長く続くと思いますが、その船自体は、技術の進歩と環境の変化により、大きく姿を変えています。最近20フィートコンテナ2万個積みの超大型(メガ)コンテナ船が登場し話題になっています。全長約400メートル、幅約59メートルにもなるそうです。高さ333メートルの東京タワーよりも長いビルのような船で、相当な迫力があります。

　このようなメガコンテナ船に積載される貨物の関係者(荷主)の数は、1万社を超えることもあります。共同海損になった場合、この膨大な数の貨物関係者から共同海損分担保証関連書類を取り付けることを想像してみてください。電子メールやIT機器が発達し、通信手段は格段に進歩していますが、1万社を超える関係者との連絡は容易ではありません。

　これまで就航しているコンテナ船でも、共同海損分担保証関連書類の取付けに、海損精算事務所で15人位のチームを立ち上げ、世界各地の提携先と連携して何とかすべての貨物関係者から書類を取り付けています。メガコンテナ船が座礁したような場合、浮揚させるために、洋上でコンテナ貨物を別の船に仮揚げする必要が生じること

第8章　ヨーク・アントワープ規則（海上運送契約で合意された共同海損精算のよりどころ）

もあり得ますが、救助技術的にかなりの困難を伴います。

メガコンテナ船の事故対応については、今後、海運、救助、保険業界で問題になるものと思います。

## 2　ヨーク・アントワープ規則って、何？

第4章「共同海損認容に関する2つの基本思想」で、2016年5月3日から6日まで世界各国の法律家や実務家が出席し万国海法会第42回国際会議が開催され、2016年ヨーク・アントワープ規則（以下、2016年YARと言います）が採択されたことをお伝えしました。これから、共同海損精算のよりどころであるヨーク・アントワープ規則について、ご説明いたしましょう。少し説明が専門的になりますが、ご容赦ください。

まず、YARの法的立場、次に、なぜ荷主がこのYARに縛られるのか。3番目に、YARはどのような過程を経て改定されるか。4番目にYARの構成。

そして最後に1994年YARと2016年YARの主な相違点について、順に見ていきましょう。

### (1) YARは条約、それとも法律？

YARは条約でも、法律でもありません。万国海法会（CMI）という各国海事法専門家の集まりが、海上運送にかかわる利害関係者の意見を聴いて採択し、見直している国際的な統一規則ですが、条約でも法律でもないのです。

また、YARは単一の規則ではなく、1994年YAR、2004年YAR、2016年YARなどのいくつかのバージョンがあります。

### (2) なぜ、船主や、荷主はこのYARに縛られるのでしょうか？

YARは国際的な統一規則なので、当然に航海関係者に適用されるものではありません。それでは、なぜ船主、荷主は、条約でも法律でもないYARという統一規則に縛られるのでしょうか。それは、まず船主が、船荷証券や用船契約といった海上運送契約書の中に「共同海損事案が生じたら、YARに従って共同海損精算を行う」と記載し、荷主がこれを承諾することによって、当事者間の合意（運送契約の一部）となっているからです。

上記2つの点の理解を深めるために、少し歴史をさかのぼりましょう。共同海損について、伝統的にイギリスは、共同安全主義（船舶が避難港に入港し安全が確保された時点で共同海損は終了するとの考え）を採用し、フランス等のヨーロッパ大陸では、航海完遂主義（当初予定していた航海が完了した時点で共同海損は終了するとの考え）を採用していました。

Ⅰ　わかりやすい共同海損

船主と荷主の国籍が異なることが多いため、国によって共同海損についての考え方が異なると、実際の精算業務に支障が生じます。

各国の共同海損の取扱いを統一するために国際会議が開かれ、1860年にグラスゴー決議（Glasgow Resolutions）、1864年にヨーク規則（York Rules）、1877年にヨーク・アントワープ規則（York-Antwerp Rules 1877）が採択されました。やっとYARが産声を上げたわけです。

当時、海事法関係者は、共同海損のルールを統一するためには、「統一共同海損法の制定」が一番望ましいと考え、この目標に向かって長年努力しました。しかし、利害関係が複雑に入り混じりなかなか目的が達成しにくいため、次善の策として、「共同海損ルールの自主的統一」、すなわち、ルールを統一し、そのルールを船主と荷主が海上運送契約に取り入れることに合意することによって、実質的な統一を達成することを目指しました。このような関係者の努力の積み重ねによって、現在では、ほとんどすべての海上運送契約にYARが取り入れられ合意されています。

(3) YARはどのような過程を経て改定されるのでしょうか？

上記のとおり、YARは長年かかって統一されたルールですが、統一されたことにより、そのルールが不変かというと、そうではありません。その後、帆船の時代から蒸気船、鋼船・発動機船への輸送用具の変化、また、そのときどきの時代の要請に応じ、YARは、1890年、1924年、1950年、1974年、1990年、1994年、2004年に改定されました。

2004年YARでは、救助報酬が共同海損に認容されないこと、事故後、避難入港中の本船船員の給料手当および食料金が共同海損に認容されないこと等、1994年YARと比べて、共同海損に認容される範囲が狭く、船主にとって受け入れがたい内容のため、ほとんど利用されていません。

せっかく新しい規則を作ったのに使われない状態は好ましくないので、万国海法会は、より一層利害関係者に受け入れられ、より利用されるようにYARを改定する作業を続けてきました。その結果、船舶や貨物といった航海関係者の合意に基づき、2016年5月ニューヨークで開催された万国海法会第42回国際会議で、2016年ヨーク・アントワープ規則（2016年YAR）が採択されました。

(4) YARの構成

YARの存在意義および現状について、ご理解いただけましたでしょうか。YARが産声を上げてから、非常に長い間維持されており、今後もその必要性は変わらないものと思いますが、そのYARの中身は、時代のニーズの変化に応じて、絶えず変わり続けています。

第8章　ヨーク・アントワープ規則（海上運送契約で合意された共同海損精算のよりどころ）

次に、YARにはどのような規定が盛り込まれているのかをご説明したいと思います。現在、最も広く利用されている1994年YARは、次の4つのパートによって構成されています。
① 解釈規定（Rule of Interpretation）：解釈の原則を定めた規定です。
② 至上規定（Rule Paramount）：その名のとおり最も重要な規定です。
③ 文字規定（Lettered Rules）：共同海損の一般原則を定めたA条からG条までの部分です。
④ 数字規定（Numbered Rules）：Ⅰ条（1条）からⅩⅩⅡ条（22条）までの部分です。

文字規定では、共同海損の一般原則が規定されており、数字規定では、具体的にどのような場合に共同海損として認容され、どのように分担されるのかという例が、規定されています。

解釈規定には、「至上規定および数字規定により規定された場合を除き、共同海損は文字規定に従い精算する」と定められており、数字規定が文字規定に優先します。

## ③ 1994年YARと2016年YARの主な相違点

それでは、現在最も広く利用されている1994年YARと、採択されたばかりの2016年YARの相違点についてご説明したいと思います。主な相違点[17]は、以下の3つです。
① 救助報酬の共同海損への認容の可否
② 共同海損の立替手数料と利息
③ 共同海損請求権の時効

1つ目は救助報酬です。船舶と貨物を救うために、救助業者に救助を依頼する方法は、あらかじめ救助報酬の総額を定めるLumpsum方式（総額協定方式）、救助船1日あたりの金額を定めたDaily Hire（日額協定方式）、そして救助報酬をあらかじめ定めないで、救助された財産の価額や救助の難易度などに基づき、後日決めるロイズ救助契約書式（ロイズ・オープン・フォーム：LOF）や日本海運集会所書式（JSEフォーム）があります。その内容について、要点を次ページの図表3に、まとめてみました。

1994年YARでは、船舶と貨物を共同の危険から救うために要した救助報酬は、救助契約の様式を問わず、すべて共同海損に認容されます。しかし、2016年YARでは、LumpsumやDaily Hireの救助契約に基づく救助報酬は、共同海損に認容されます

---

[17] 改定内容の詳細を知りたい方は、東京海上日動火災保険株式会社ホームページ「マリンニュース No.202（2016年6月6日）共同海損に関する新規則『2016年ヨーク・アントワープ規則』の成立」をご覧ください。

**図表3** 救助報酬の共同海損への認容の可否

| 救助契約 | 救助依頼者 | 救助報酬支払義務者 | 1994年YAR | 2016年YAR |
|---|---|---|---|---|
| LumpsumまたはDaily Hire | 船主 | 船主が救助報酬全額の支払義務を負う。 | 共同海損に認容される。 | 共同海損に認容される。 |
| ロイズ救助契約書式または日本海運集会所書式 | 船長または船主 | 船舶、貨物などの救われた財産の所有者が、単独別個に自己の救助報酬分担額について支払義務を負う。 | 共同海損に認容される。 | 被救助価額と共同海損負担価額に重大な差がある場合などを除き、共同海損に認容されない。 |

が、ロイズ救助契約書式（LOF）や日本海運集会所書式（JSEフォーム）に基づく救助報酬は、共同海損事故の後に別の海難事故が発生し、被救助価額と共同海損負担価額に重大な差が生じた場合や、船舶や貨物が重大な差異のある水準で、救助報酬を支払った場合などを除き、共同海損に認容されません[18]。

2つ目は、共同海損の立替手数料と利息です。内容は図表4のとおりです。

3つ目は、共同海損請求権の時効です。1994年YARには、時効に関する規定はなかったので、海上運送契約で規定された準拠法に基づき、共同海損請求権の時効を判断します。準拠法が英法で、貨物関係者から共同海損分担保証関連書類を入手している場合は、1980年Limitation Actに基づき、共同海損精算書発行から6年で時効が完成します。日本法が適用される場合は、2018年改正商法第812条（改正前第798条）に基づき、共同海損精算書発行から1年で時効が完成します。

2016年YARでは、共同海損精算書発行から1年で時効となり、いかなる場合も、航海終了後6年で、訴訟を提起しない限り、共同海損分担請求権が消滅する、との規定が新設されました[19]。

---

[18] 船舶と貨物を共同の危険から救うために要した費用である救助報酬は、契約のいかんを問わず、YAR A条に基づき共同海損に認容されますが、2016年YARでは、共同海損精算の迅速化、省力化のために、航海関係者間の「妥協」（compromise）が成立し、このような規定になりました。何が重大な差異（significant differences）になるかは、共同海損精算人が、事案ごとに決めることになります。

[19] コンテナ船の場合は、共同海損精算書の発行に、事故後5年以上、各貨物関係者からの分担金の回収に2年以上を要することもあります。2016年YARがそのまま適用されると、共同海損分担請求権の時効の問題に直面することが考えられます。

**図表4** 共同海損立替手数料および利息

| | 1994年 YAR | 2016年 YAR |
|---|---|---|
| 立替手数料 | 共同海損支出費用の2％ | 廃止 |
| 利　息 | 共同海損支出費用について支払日から精算書発行日から3か月後まで年7％（単利） | 共同海損支出費用について支払日から精算書発行日から3か月後まで、共同海損精算通貨の各暦年の最初の銀行取引日のICE LIBOR<sup>(注)</sup>12か月物の利率に4％を加えた利率（単利） |
| | | 2017年の適用利率は以下のとおり<br>　米ドル　年利5.689％<br>　日本円　年利4.12771％<br>　ユーロ　年利3.91357％<br>その後、毎年別の金利が適用される |

(注) ICE LIBORは、インターコンチネンタル取引所におけるロンドン銀行間金利で、世界的な短期金利の指標。

### 4 今後の見通し

1974年YARから1994年YARへの移行に10年以上の歳月を要しました。したがって、今後10年以上、1994年YARと2016年YARが併存していくことが見込まれます。

2016年YARが適用される場合でも、ロイズ救助契約書式や、日本海運集会所書式に基づき、すべての関係者との救助報酬が決まるまで、共同海損の精算が終了しない状況は、変わりません。

また共同海損分担請求権の時効期間が1994年YARと比べて短く、実務上問題となることが予想されるので、この点について万国海法会で論議、対応されるもの、と思います。

# 第9章

# 共同海損の基本形と代換費用

## 1 くまモンの生みの親

　私の母の郷里は、真珠の養殖、鯛、車海老、ポンカン、デコポンや、イルカウォッチングで有名な熊本県天草市です。当時東京の実家に下宿していた大学生のいとこの母（私の伯母）が天草で旅館をやっていたので、そのいとこに連れられ、小2と小5の夏休みに天草に遊びに行きました。東京駅から寝台特急みずほに乗って、翌日昼過ぎにようやく熊本に着きました。きれいな海、川、山があり、大好きな昆虫もたくさんいる天草の自然を満喫しました。

　その時、4歳下のいとこの小山薫堂君ともよく遊びました。彼とはその時以来の付き合いになります。彼はある大学を受験したのですが、残念ながらその大学とは縁がなく、たまたま友人が別の大学の芸術学部の願書を持っていたので、その願書をもらって放送学科を受験し、晴れて合格、上京しました。そして在学中に、生涯の師となる吉田照美氏に出会い、放送作家になりました。

　私が就職しニューヨークで研修している時、彼が遊びに来たので、2人でヘリコプターに乗り、30分ほどマンハッタンの摩天楼上空や、自由の女神周辺を遊覧し、すばらしい夜景を楽しむことができました。

　その後、彼は、映画「おくりびと」の脚本を書き、アカデミー賞外国語映画賞をもらい、九州新幹線開業で熊本が通過駅にならないように、との想いを込めて「くまモン」をプロデュースしました。くまモンの顔は、どことなく薫堂君に似ています。

　彼が最近言った忘れられない言葉をご紹介します。

　「人生に無駄なことは1つもなく、知らず知らずのうちに常にベストな選択をしている」

　奥が深い言葉ですね。

　もし彼が最初に受けた大学に合格していたら、「おくりびと」の静かな感動や、愛らしくみんなを笑顔にする「くまモン」は生まれなかったのです。

## 2　ベストな選択

　常にベストな選択をする。これは、共同海損事故が発生した後の航海関係者の選択にも、当てはまります。船舶と貨物が共同の危険にさらされる状況はさまざまで、場所、時期、気象、船体の損傷状態や積載された貨物の量などによって、船舶と貨物の共同の安全を確保するための手段がいくつか考えられますが、どのような場合でも、選択肢の中から、状況に応じたベストな選択（判断）をする。また安全が確保された後も、仕向け港までの航海を成し遂げるためにいくつかある選択肢から、同様に状況に応じたベストな選択を行うことになります。

　多くの場合、船主が、船舶と貨物双方の安全を考えてベストな判断を下し実行しますが、共同海損という船主と荷主が合意した衡平な（バランスのとれた）分担の仕組みでは、実際に採られた手段とその結果生じた費用を「共同海損特有の物差し」で測り、航海関係者間の衡平な分担の算定（共同海損の精算）を行います。

　共同海損の仕組みでは、まず、船舶と貨物を共同の危険から救うため、言い換えれば、船舶と貨物の両方が全損になってしまうことを防ぐために、共同海損行為が採られます。したがって、共同海損行為による損害や費用は、救われた船舶や貨物といった財産の総額が限度になり、救われた財産の価額に応じて、船舶や貨物が分担します。

　そして、共同海損事案では、船舶と貨物の共同の安全が確保された後に、仕向け港までの航海を完遂するためにかかる費用についても、いくつかのシナリオの中からベストな選択が行われます。共同海損として、いくら認容されるかを算定するために、別の実現可能なシナリオを考え、この「基本形」のシナリオにかかる費用を限度に、実際に採られた手段に要した費用が、共同海損に認容されます。

　このように実際に採られた手段にかかる費用は、「基本形」にかかる費用を限度に、共同海損に認容されます。耳慣れない言葉でしょうが、実際にかかった費用を、「基本形」に対する「代換費用」（代わりの費用）として、共同海損に認容すると言います。

　これから、この「基本形」と「代換費用」について、ご説明したいと思います。「代換費用」は共同海損特有の考え方なので、少しわかりにくいかもしれませんが、理解しておくべき大切なポイントですので、じっくり読んでいただけると、共同海損の全体像を把握するのに役立つものと思います。

## 3　共同海損の基本形

　共同海損の基本形と選択肢（代換費用）について、図表5（次ページ）にまとめましたので、この表をご覧いただきながら、お読みください。

I　わかりやすい共同海損

**図表5**　共同海損事故発生後の航海の流れ

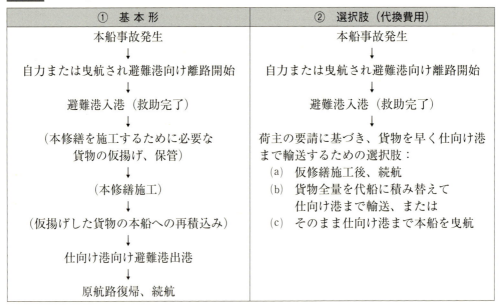

　海上運送人は、運送契約上、運賃を収得する代わりに貨物を無事に仕向け港まで運送する義務を負っていますので、船主は、共同海損になるような大事故が発生した場合には、まず自力もしくは救助船を手配して、本船を避難港に入港させ、安全を確保したうえで、航海継続のために必要とされる検査や修繕を行い、本船で貨物を仕向け港まで運送することを考えます。これが、共同海損の基本形です。

　運送契約上、航海が遅延しても、運送人としては、避難港で修繕を施工する等して、本船を続航可能な状態に復旧して、貨物を仕向け港まで輸送すれば、契約上の義務を果たしたことになります。

　私の共同海損精算の師である故近藤敬三氏は、この基本形に沿って事故対応すれば、1974年または1994年ヨーク・アントワープ規則に基づき、航海完遂のために余分に要した費用の大半は、共同海損に認容される、とよく話していました。そのとおりだと思います。

## 4　代船輸送された場合の具体例

　共同海損では、前述したとおり、事故後本船で仕向け港まで続航する基本形が採られる場合のほか、実際にその他の手段が採られることによって支出された仮修繕費、代船輸送費用や、仕向け港までの曳航費も、基本形を採ったとすれば、共同海損に認容されたであろう費用を限度に、共同海損に認容されます。

　避難港における本修繕が長期間になることが見込まれ、荷主の要請に基づき、早期

に貨物を仕向け港まで輸送するために、避難港で、貨物全量を代船に積み替えて、仕向け港まで輸送することがあります。具体例を挙げて、ご説明しましょう。

貨物船A（17,999総トン）は、鋼材26,000トンを積載し千葉／ロサンゼルス間を航行中、館山沖で座礁しました。座礁の結果、船底の広い範囲にわたり亀裂等の損害が生じました。幸い本船は、自力航行が可能でしたので、曳航されずに自力で最寄りの本修繕が可能な港、横浜に避難入港しました。損傷を検査し、造船所と協議した結果、ロサンゼルスまでの航海を完遂するためには、鋼材26,000トン全量を横浜で本船から仮揚げし、修繕ドックに入って、本修繕を施工する必要があることがわかりました。また、横浜で本修繕完了後、本船で続航すると、横浜に2か月間留まらなければならないということもわかりました。

本修繕施工後、本船で続航する選択肢を採る場合には、図表6のとおり、貨物の仮揚げ、保管および本船への再積込み費用の合計1億4,550万円が共同海損に認容されます。これが共同海損の基本形の費用です。

**図表6** 代船輸送された場合の具体例

| 基本形（避難港で本修繕施工後、続航した場合） | |
|---|---:|
| 鋼材26,000トンの仮揚げ費用 | ¥57,000,000 |
| 鋼材26,000トンの保管費用（2か月分） | ¥31,500,000 |
| 仮揚げ、保管した鋼材26,000トンの本船への再積込み費用 | ¥57,000,000 |
| 共同海損認容見込み額合計 | **¥145,500,000** A |

| 荷主の要請に基づき、貨物全量を代船輸送した場合 | |
|---|---:|
| 鋼材26,000トンの仮揚げ費用 | ¥57,000,000 |
| 鋼材26,000トンの保管費用（1週間分） | ¥3,500,000 |
| 仮揚げ、保管した鋼材26,000トンの代船への積込み費用 | ¥57,000,000 |
| 代船の用船料 | ¥30,000,000 |
| 代船の仕向け港港費 | ¥1,000,000 |
| 代船輸送関連費用 | **¥148,500,000** B |

| | |
|---|---:|
| 事故地点から仕向け港で貨物を揚げ切るまでの期間の本船船員の給料手当および食料金 | ¥6,000,000 |
| 上記期間に消費されたであろう本船燃料代および清水代 | ¥3,000,000 |
| 本船の仕向け港港費 | ¥1,000,000 |
| 本船の通常航海所要費用見込み額 | **¥10,000,000** C |

| | |
|---|---:|
| 正味代船輸送関連費用 （B－C） | ¥138,500,000 D |
| 代換費用としての共同海損認容額（A ≧ D） | **¥138,500,000** |

一方、荷主の要請に基づいて、貨物を早くロサンゼルスに運ぶべく、代船により輸送するという選択肢を採ると、代船輸送に伴う費用として1億4,850万円が見込まれます。また、代船輸送した結果、事故地点の館山沖から仕向け港ロサンゼルスまで本船は航行しないで済むので、この間の本船の通常航海所要費用が節約されます。この費用として1,000万円が見込まれました。

　代船輸送関連費用1億4,850万円から、本船の通常航海所要費用見込み額1,000万円を控除した正味代船輸送関連費用1億3,850万円は、横浜で本修繕を施工した場合に共同海損に認められたであろう貨物26,000トンの仮揚げ、保管および本船への再積込み費用の見込み額1億4,550万円、すなわち、基本形の費用を限度に共同海損に認容されます。したがって、この場合、正味代船輸送費用1億3,850万円の全額が代換費用として共同海損に認容されます[20]。

　少し複雑になりましたが、どのような費用が共同海損に認められるのか、また基本形と異なった対応が採られた場合に、どこまで、基本形の代わりに支出された費用が代換費用として共同海損に認められるのか、ご理解いただけましたでしょうか。

　船主はいつもベストな選択をしますが、そのベストな選択にかかる費用は、共同海損の仕組みに基づき、整理、精算され、船舶や貨物といった航海関係者間で衡平に分担されます。

| トピックス5 | 船貨不分離協定（Non-Separation Agreement） |

　共同海損は、船舶や貨物といった共同危険団体が、運命共同体であるがゆえに成立する仕組みであり、貨物が本船から分離（揚げ荷）されると、その貨物はこの運命共同体から抜けてしまいます。

　この点について、『共同海損の理論と実務――1994年ヨーク・アントワープ規則の解説』[21]にとてもわかりやすく解説されています（以下引用）。

　「船舶が事故により避難港に入り修繕を行う場合には、積荷の仮揚、保管、再積込の費用や、停泊中の船費等の共同海損費用が増大するという問題のほかに、積荷の保管中の危険や、受荷主への積荷の引渡の遅れ、という問題が生じる。そのような問題を回避する対策として、船主が代船を手配し、積荷を目的地まで継送することがしばしば行われる。

　その場合、共同海損本来の考え方からいくと、船貨分離によって共同危険団体が崩れることとなるため、その時点で共同海損が終了し、荷主は積荷をより早く受取るという便宜を得たうえに、船主が支出した修繕期間中の燃料や船員の給食料等の共同海損費用につい

---

[20]　正味代船輸送関連費用が1億5,000万円であれば、1億4,550万円が代換費用として共同海損に認容され、450万円は共同海損に認容されません。

[21]　東京海上火災保険株式会社海損部編著『共同海損の理論と実務――1994年ヨーク・アントワープ規則の解説』（有斐閣、1995）78ページから79ページ。

ては分担を免れるという、はなはだ不公平な事態が生じる場合がある。

そこで、このような不公平を是正するため、船主が荷主から船貨不分離協定を取り付け、船貨が分離しても共同海損は終了しないものと見なし、あたかも代船輸送がなかったかのように共同海損の精算を行う旨の協定を行うことが世界的慣行となっていた。

最も広く行われていた標準的なフォームである British Standard Form 1967 は次の通りである。

（中略）

〔訳〕「本船の積荷の全部または一部が、一隻の他船、数隻の他船またはその他の輸送用具によって当初の仕向地に継送された場合の共同海損の権利義務は、かかる継送により影響されないことに合意し、この点については、かかる継送を行うことなく元の船舶で航海を継続した場合に適用される法律または運送契約の下で許されるところと同様の立場に関係当事者を置くことを目的とするものである。

関係財貨の共同海損分担の基準は、仕向地へ到着前に売却その他の方法により処分された場合を除き、当初の仕向地において引渡された時の価額とする。但し、積荷が全く本船によって継送されなかった場合は、本船は、積荷の揚切り時の実際の価額に基づいて分担する」（引用終わり）

船貨不分離協定の実務上の効果は、以下の2つです。
① 正味代船輸送費用等の船貨分離後の共同海損費用についても、貨物が分担する。
② 修繕完了までに消費された燃料代、清水代ならびに船員の給料手当、食料金を共同海損として認容する。

1990年修正1974年ヨーク・アントワープ規則までは、いちいち船貨不分離協定を貨物関係者から取り付ける必要がありましたが、同様の趣旨の規定が1994年ヨーク・アントワープ規則G条第3パラグラフに挿入されたことにより、1994年ヨーク・アントワープ規則または2016年ヨーク・アントワープ規則が適用される場合には、別途船貨不分離協定を取り付ける必要がなくなりました。

# 第10章

## 共同海損の精算書作成とコンサルティング

### 1 世界中の人たちがシェアできるもの

　皆さん、絵はお好きですか。16世紀ネーデルランドの巨匠ピーテル・ブリューゲルの最高傑作「バベルの塔」をご覧になった方もいらっしゃるかもしれません。港町に立つ10数階建てのレンガ造りの塔、ものすごい迫力で描かれていますね。バベルの塔の物語は、昔人類は、皆同じ言葉を話していたが、天まで届く高い塔を建てようとして、神の怒りにふれ、塔が崩れ、言葉もバラバラになり、意思疎通が難しくなってしまった、というものです。人間の傲慢さを批判していると言われています。

　でも、ご安心ください。私たちは、言葉は通じなくても、スポーツや音楽を通して、世界中の人たちと、楽しく熱い時間と想いを共有（シェア）することができます。私の知人の有名なパーカッション奏者がいつも言っていることなのですが、人類が誕生した時から、人は、身近な物を打楽器にしてリズムをとり、歌い、踊ってきたのです。歌や踊りには、原始時代からお互いの気持ちを通じ合わせる力があります。

　私は、サルサの次にミュージカルが大好きで、とくにアンドリュー・ロイド・ウェバー作「オペラ座の怪人」を、劇場で何度も見ました。皆さんご存知のとおり、パリ・オペラ座のコーラスガールのクリスティーヌを、主役にしようとオペラ座の地下に住む怪人が、彼女の歌のコーチになり、主役にするのですが、最後に悲劇的な結末が待っています。

　私の5歳の息子も歌が大好きで、音楽教室で習った「ロンドン橋」などの曲をドレミで歌いながら、一緒にピアノの両手弾きの練習をしています。音楽が大好きな大人になれるといいな、と思っています。

　言語、人種、宗教が異なり、場所、時間、世代が違っても、踊りや音楽は、これらの違いを乗り越えて、世界中の人たちが共有できるすばらしい手段だと思います。

　もちろん、ここでお伝えしたいのは、少し強引かもしれませんが、共同海損も、立場が異なっていても、世界中の人たちがシェアできる仕組みだということです。これから、共同海損が、より多くの皆さんに広く理解していただくための工夫を、関係者が行っていることをご説明し、また、個々の事案をよりスムーズに解決するために

は、やはり関係者の皆さんと共同海損精算人との間で、タイムリーに打ち合わせること、また、必要に応じて、共同海損精算人同士でも事案に対する考え方について意見交換することが有益であることをご説明したい、と思います。

## 2 共同海損に関する万国海法会（CMI）ガイドライン

2016年ヨーク・アントワープ規則の成立にあわせて、2016年5月新たに共同海損に関するCMIガイドライン（本書Vに全文収録）が採択されました。この中で、初めて共同海損精算人の役割について規定されました。このガイドラインに法的拘束力はありませんが、普段あまり共同海損になじみがない共同海損の利害関係者にとって、わかりやすく共同海損の基本原理や、精算手続きの概要について説明しており、ご一読されることをお勧めします。

この中で、誰に委嘱されたかにかかわらず、共同海損精算人は、共同の航海団体を構成するすべての利害関係者に対して公正に対応すべく、中立、独立した立場でその職務を遂行する、と明記されました。

通常、船主が共同海損の精算を委嘱しますが、船舶関係者からいくら言われても、「ヨーク・アントワープ規則に基づいて、貨物にきちんと説明できないような費用や損害は、共同海損として貨物に分担を求めることはできませんよ」、と私も共同海損精算人として、説明することがあります。

今までも、共同海損精算人は、ヨーク・アントワープ規則に基づき、公平公正に対応してきましたが、このことが改めてガイドラインに明記された意味をよく認識し、共同海損精算人として、船舶や貨物といった航海関係者の皆さんにとって、フェアなシェアとなることを、心がけていきたいと思います。

## 3 共同海損精算人のコンサルティング業務

さて、最初と最後が肝心、という言葉がありますが、この言葉は、共同海損についても当てはまります。

とくに共同海損になるような事故が発生した当初と、共同海損分担額を支払う前に、船舶や貨物などの航海関係者の皆さんが、共同海損精算人に気軽に相談することが非常に有益と思います。私が共同海損の精算を始めた30数年前は、たいていの事案で船舶の価額が、貨物の価額を上回っていましたが、最近、貨物の価額の方が船舶の価額よりも多い、すなわち、船舶の共同海損分担額よりも貨物の共同海損分担額が多くなる事案が増えています。実際に、分担割合が、船舶が10％、貨物が90％というコンテナ船の事案もあります。

このような事情から、貨物関係者にとっても、共同海損精算人に相談する重要性は増しているものと思います。

### 4 事案のより良い解決のために対話が大切

英米の海損精算人は、事案の内容が少し複雑になると、どんなに経験豊富な海損精算人でも、また、自分自身の対応方針にある程度自信を持っている場合でも、同僚の海損精算人に、「ぼくはこう思うけど、君はどう思う」と尋ねます。このような会話をプロの海損精算人同士でしながら、迅速に事案の適切な対応方針を決めていきます。

これは、自分の考えの正しさを確認する意味合いもありますが、他のより経験を積んだ海損精算人から異なる見方や考え方を学ぶ絶好の機会でもあります。

共同海損精算人には、とてもフランクで親切な人が多く、具体的な事案で、私も1対1の対話を通して、非常に多くのことを学びました。

日本では、保険会社の海損船舶の担当者の皆さんが、実質的に英米の海損精算人の役割の一部も担っています。担当する海難事故の対応で判断に迷うような場合には、ぜひ気軽に共同海損精算人に相談されることをお勧めします。とくに事故発生当初、事案の見立てをする段階で、共同海損精算人との対話を通して、事実関係を確認し問題を整理しながら、事案の最適解を見つけることに役に立つと思います。

最近、今治からシンガポールに転勤された海損船舶担当者から、今治時代と同様、気軽に電話やメールをいただきます。彼と対話しながら、ヨーク・アントワープ規則に基づいて、どこまで共同海損に認容されるかを一緒に考えていくことは、共同海損精算人として、楽しいものです。

### 5 共同海損精算書の作成、発行および決済

次に、共同海損精算人の一番大切な仕事である共同海損精算書の作成、発行および決済（共同海損分担額の回収）について、ご説明したいと思います。

共同海損事故発生直後の初期対応が終了すると、共同海損精算人は、船舶、貨物、燃料などの関係者から収集した書類に基づき、共同海損事故に関連して支出されたさまざまな費用や損害について、共同海損としていくら認められ、共同海損行為の結果、救われた、船舶、貨物といった利害関係者がそれぞれいくら共同海損分担額を支払うべきかを記した冊子を作成、発行します。

この冊子が共同海損精算書です。精算というたった2文字の作業ですが、多くの費用が支出された場合には、バウチャー（支払関連書類）がバインダー10冊近くになる

こともあり、共同海損精算人として、本船の動静、救助の進展状況などをつぶさに検証して、どの時点までの費用を共同海損の対象とするかという検討も行います。

石炭や穀物を運ぶばら積み貨物船等の貨物関係者が少ない場合には、印刷・製本した共同海損精算書を請求書と共に、共同海損精算人から、貨物等の関係者に送付しています。他方、貨物関係者が数千以上になるようなコンテナ船の事案では、共同海損精算事務所のウェブサイトに共同海損精算書のpdf版を貼り付け、貨物関係者がユーザー名とパスワードを入力し、共同海損精算書をダウンロードすることが多くなっています。

共同海損精算書の冒頭には、事故の概要、共同海損精算に適用されるヨーク・アントワープ規則、主な共同海損認容額についての共同海損精算人の説明があります。この部分（Executive Summary; Adjuster's Explanatory Notes）を読めば、共同海損精算内容の全体像または概要が理解できます。まさに共同海損精算のエッセンスであり、共同海損精算人の力量が問われる部分と言えます。

ところで、共同海損精算書の作成には、どのくらいの時間がかかるのでしょうか。原油、石炭、穀物等の荷口が少ないばら積み貨物船の共同海損精算には、1年から3年ぐらい、コンテナ船のように荷口が数千を超えるような場合は、5年以上かかる場合が多い、と思います。最近話題のコンテナ2万個積みの超大型コンテナ船で、もし共同海損が起これば、15人程度の特別チームを立ち上げても、共同海損精算に10年以上の歳月を要するかもしれません。

共同海損精算人は、通常船主の依頼に基づき、共同海損精算書に記載した船舶、貨物などの共同海損分担額を請求しますが、この分担額の回収作業は数か月で終わる場合もありますが、コンテナ船の場合には、2年以上かかることもあります。

## 6 おわりに

第1章から第10章までお読みいただくと、共同海損の全体像のご理解に役立つものと思います。保険毎日新聞は、幅広い保険関連の皆さんが購読されており、できるだけわかりやすい記述を心がけました。

共同海損精算人の一番大切な役割は、海上運送契約に定められた規則に基づき、公正公平な立場で、共同海損行為によって救われた船舶、貨物、コンテナ、燃料といった各航海利害関係者の利益を調整（アジャスト）し、早期に事案を解決（セトル）することだと信じています。

今後も、保険毎日新聞、損害保険事業総合研究所の損保講座、日本海損精算人協会主催セミナーなどの場で、皆さんにわかりやすく共同海損の考え方を、ご説明していきたいと思っています。引き続き、どうぞよろしくお願いいたします。

Ⅰ　わかりやすい共同海損

　皆さんの航海の無事を祈りつつ、共同海損の仕組みについての解説を終わります。最後まで、お読みいただき、ありがとうございました。

---

**トピックス6**　　過失と共同海損の関係

　貨物保険者は Average Guarantee を発行していても、共同海損の事故原因が本船の発航時不堪航によるものであると合理的に主張できる場合には、貨物の共同海損分担金の支払いを拒否することができます。このような場合には、その旨を書面で海損精算人に通知します。

　船主は、発航時不堪航を理由に、共同海損の分担を拒否する旨の貨物保険者からの回答を添えて、貨物の分担金の支払いを加入しているPIクラブに請求することになります[※]。

　ただし、LOF（ロイズ・オープン・フォーム）等の救助費については、船舶や貨物といった各分担利益が、単独別個に救助業者に対して支払義務を負いますので、本船の発航時不堪航を理由に、貨物保険者が救助費分担額の支払いを拒否することはできません。

　※ PIクラブの Indemnity で保険金支払いの対象になります。

◆1994年ヨーク・アントワープ規則D条◆
「犠牲または費用を生ぜしめた事故が、航海団体の当事者のうちの一人の過失に起因した場合でも、共同海損の分担請求権は影響を受けない。ただし、この場合その当事者に対しかかる過失に対し求償（remedies）または抗弁（defences）することを妨げない。」

# II

# A Clear Guide to General Average

Eiichi Nakada
Average Adjuster

# Chapter 1

# What is General Average, or GA?

What do you imagine from the word of General Average, or simply GA? Although you might have heard the word, GA, you may not have a concrete idea, or even if you would like to study GA, you might hesitate to read thick hardcover books.

You may recall a one-time best-seller 'If the world were a village of 100 people'. Adjustment of General Average is just like that. Only about 100 active GA adjusters in the world are currently preparing formal Adjustments of General Average. I am one of three GA adjusters in Japan, and shall explain to you the basic principles and practice of General Average. From now on I will use the word, GA, instead of General Average.

Let us begin the history of GA. GA is a natural law of the sea which was borne nearly 3,000 years ago. GA has a very long history, which system existed even before Marine Insurance.

From the fourth to third centuries BC, the Rhodes had been a very prosperous trading centre in the east Mediterranean Sea. The Rhodian law decrees that if, in order to lighten a ship, a merchandise has been thrown overboard (this is called 'jettison'), such merchandise should be replaced by the contribution of all, since it has been given up for all.

The same statement was found in Japanese oldest sea code in the fifteenth century, 'Kaisen Shikimoku (shipping laws)'.

In ancient Greek and Roman periods since communication tools had not been developed, once in a while in addition to the shipowners, the cargo owners or their agents took onboard a sailing ship as supercargo (a representative of the cargo owners on board the ship who is responsible for supervising the cargo). When she encountered the heavy weather, with the consent of the cargo owners or their agents, a part of the cargo was thrown overboard. Once the ship safely arrived at destination, the captain asked for contributions to all the saved parties on the ship for the sacrificed cargo. This is considered to be the genesis of Adjustment of GA.

GA is a very old system peculiar to carriage by sea, which still works effectively to balance the interests among the common maritime transport on the same ship, and has been keeping a very close relationship with the shipowners, the ship managers, the charterers, the cargo owners and the forwarders.

Although 'the principle of equitable distribution' in GA is very simple as stated in the Rhodian law, it is very difficult to explain the details of the whole system. I would like to explain to you the points step by step in accordance with the following themes:

① What is the general image of General Average?
② What should we do when the General Average accident happened?
③ What will happen if the cargo was not insured?
④ Which expenses are allowed in General Average?
⑤ Which losses are allowed in General Average?
⑥ What are the York-Antwerp Rules?
⑦ What are the job and the roles of GA adjusters?

By reading through this article with interest, you will learn the general principles and practice of GA, which will help you, when you are involved with the ship accident, and will benefit all members of international trade as their risk management.

# Chapter 2

# What is the general image of General Average?

First of all, let me give you general idea of General Average.

General Average is often called as GA from its initials.

The York-Antwerp Rules 1994 (abbreviated as YAR 1994 hereinafter) have been widely adopted in the contracts of sea carriage such as Bills of Lading and Charter Parties as the standard international rule for adjusting GA.

Rule A, YAR 1994[1] defines GA as follows:

"There is a general average act when, and only when, any extraordinary sacrifice or expenditure is intentionally and reasonably made or incurred for the common safety for the purpose of preserving from the peril the property involved in a common maritime adventure."

Now, in what situation GA happens. Let me take a concrete example:

During a voyage, a maritime accident such as collision, stranding or fire, etc. may happen on a ship laden with cargo. If no action is taken by the master or the crew, the ship and the cargo will sink or break up, and become a total loss in the end. Under such a dangerous situation, to save the ship and the cargo from the common danger, the master may request for a salvage assistance.

A salvage tug boat arrives at the accident scene. Having inspected damage conditions of the ship, she is towed into the nearest safe port (which is called "a port of refuge"). Then the necessary repairs, which enable the ship to continue the intended voyage, are carried out at the port, and she arrives at destination.

In such a case, salvage remuneration incurred to save the vessel and the cargo, the port of refuge expenses due to the ship's emergency call, etc. are allowed in GA. These

---

(1) Comparing to the Rhodian law which was explained in Chapter 1; "if, in order to lighten a ship, a merchandise has been thrown overboard, such merchandise should be replaced by the contribution of all, since it has been given up for all.", the sentence becomes longer here, and in addition to any sacrifice, expenditure is also the subject of GA. But please feel at ease, I shall explain to you more details of YAR in my later chapter.

Chapter 2  What is the general image of General Average?

GA disbursements are shared among the ship and the cargo, and borne by them based on each saved value[2] at the end of the voyage (or at the completion of discharge of the cargo from the vessel) at destination.

From this example you can roughly get the basic idea on GA system. If you need to explain what GA system is, you could answer GA is a system through which the expenditures or losses to save the ship and the cargo are borne by the ship and the cargo according to each saved value at the destination.

In other words when only the ship or the cargo is saved, there is no GA. In such a case, no action is taken for the common safety of the ship and the cargo, but only for saving either the ship or the cargo. Only when both the ship and the cargo are saved and arrive at destination, there is GA.

The entire work to assess GA expenditures and/or losses and to allocate (distribute) them among the saved properties is called GA Adjustment. Let me take a brief example how GA is adjusted.

Let's say, salvage remuneration allowed in GA is JPY300,000,000.

The net arrived value (saved value) of the ship at the end of the voyage at destination is JPY600,000,000 and the same for the cargo is JPY400,000,000.

In such case the ship and the cargo will pay (contribute) the GA as follows:

| Contributing Interests (Saved interests by GA act) | Contributory Value of GA (Saved amount) | Proportion of GA (Amount to be borne) |
|---|---|---|
| Ship | JPY 600,000,000 | JPY 180,000,000 |
| Cargo | JPY 400,000,000 | JPY 120,000,000 |
| Totals | JPY 1,000,000,000 | (Total amount of GA allowances) JPY 300,000,000 |

Percentage of GA* at 30%

* Percentage of GA is a proportion of the total allowed GA expenditures out of the aggregate amount of the saved properties such as the ship and the cargo as a result of GA act, which shows at what percentage of the amount of all the saved properties GA should be borne. From the GA percentage you can grasp the size of GA case.

---

(2) The saved value is called "GA Contributory Value" which is a base amount to contribute GA. The amount to be paid by the saved properties such as the ship and the cargo, etc. is called "Proportion of GA".

## II  A Clear Guide to General Average

This is a typical example of GA. It is my great pleasure if you could understand how the GA expenditures, such as salvage remuneration intentionally incurred for the common safety of the ship and the cargo, are borne by the saved properties, and meaning of the several technical words, which are sometimes very similar to each other and can be easily mistaken, in assessment of proportions of GA.

# Chapter 3

# What should we do when the GA accident happens?

In Chapter 2 you have grasped general idea of General Average; in what situation GA takes place and is declared, how GA is assessed (adjusted) and allocated among the saved properties.

GA system universally applies both to the bulk carriers which carry, for example, crude oil, iron ore or coal, consisting only small numbers of the entire cargo owners, and to the container ships, only one of which may involve more than ten thousand cargo interests.

Now, when GA accident occurs, what will happen and what should we do?

When GA accident happens, in the first instance the shipowners appoint GA Adjuster and declare GA to all the cargo interests (the cargo owners) onboard the vessel. This procedure is identical irrespective of the numbers of the cargoes involved. By declaring GA[3] the shipowners inform the cargo owners, who are not usually on board the ship, that GA accident happens, and in due course the cargo interests will be asked to pay their share of the GA disbursements which were incurred for the common safety of the ship and the cargo.

GA Declaration is thunderbolt to the cargo owners. Now, how should they deal with such a situation?

Further to declaring GA, very clearly and precisely speaking, the shipowners request the cargo owners as follows:

① Please accept the GA declaration and promise to pay proportion of GA in due course
② Please let us have security to ensure the payment of the cargo proportion of GA when the GA Adjustment is issued, and
③ Please let us know the cargo value in order for us to adjust the GA properly.

In other words, very rigidly speaking, the cargo owners are requested to provide the

---

(3) Notice of GA declaration is usually called as GA Declaration Letter.

shipowners or the GA Adjusters with GA Securities; the following documents prior to taking delivery of the cargo at destination:

① Average Bond to be signed by the cargo receivers:
Average Bond is a document in which the cargo receivers promise to pay their GA proportion when the GA Adjustment is issued.

② Letter of Guarantee or Average Guarantee to be signed by the cargo underwriters:
Letter of Guarantee is often called as Average Guarantee, in which the cargo underwriters promise to pay the GA contribution of their insured cargo when the GA Adjustment is issued.

③ Valuation Form[4] to be signed by the cargo receivers.
Valuation Form is a declaration of the cargo value by the cargo receivers.

④ Commercial Invoice Copy of the cargo
Copy of Commercial Invoice is a material to ascertain the CIF value of the cargo which becomes the basis for the GA contributory value of the cargo.

The shipowners inform the cargo owners, at the same time, that they will not deliver the cargo at destination unless the above GA Securities have been provided to the shipowners or the GA Adjusters because the shipowners have a very strong legal right to hold the cargo, which is called as maritime lien.

Although you might know the above steps, since GA declaration and the wordings of GA Securities are written in unfamiliar long wordings, it is not easy for the cargo owners to understand the necessary procedures precisely.

Well then, what the cargo owners should do?

The answer is very simple. You should advise the cargo owners that upon receipt of the GA Declaration Letter, they should contact the cargo insurers as soon as possible.

---

(4) Recently some GA adjusters insert the wordings of Valuation Form in Average Bond to reduce the paper work.

# Chapter 4

# When a cargo is not insured, the cargo owner may get involved in trouble.

In Chapter 3 I have explained that when GA accident happens the shipowners appoint GA Adjuster and declare GA to all the cargo owners onboard the vessel. On the other hand, upon receipt of GA Declaration Letter, in the first instance the cargo owners should contact to their cargo underwriters. Can you figure out in such an immediate advice to the cargo underwriters is essential?

The most painful thing for the cargo owners is, unless they are able to submit the GA Securities[5] as requested by the GA Adjusters, they are not allowed to receive their cargo at destination.

Then, why is the notice to the cargo underwriters the easiest way? Because, when submitting the GA Securities in practice, the role of the cargo insurers is crucial.

As soon as the cargo owners receive GA Declaration Letter from the shipowners or their agents, they should transmit it to the cargo insurers by email together with the requested forms of Average Guarantee, Average Bond and Valuation Form.

It is necessary for the cargo receivers to write down and sign the Average Bond and Valuation Form. If the contents and/or how to write down are unclear, their cargo underwriters are very welcome to explain the details to the cargo receivers.

In addition to these, it is perfect for the cargo receivers to send their cargo insurers the relevant original cargo Insurance Policy together with copies of Commercial Invoice and Bill of Lading (and Voyage Charter Party, if any).

Then, how will the cargo insurers cope with the situation? They will respond to many questions from the cargo owners, and, after having obtained the above documents, issue

---

(5) As I explained in Chapter 3, GA Securities consist of the following four documents; Average Bond and Valuation Form to be signed by the cargo receivers, Letter of Guarantee (Average Guarantee) to be signed by the cargo insurers and Commercial Invoice Copy.

*63*

Letter of Guarantee (Average Guarantee) [6] addressed to the shipowners.

Once the cargo receivers and the cargo insurers have submitted the above GA Securities [7] to the shipowners or GA Adjusters, the cargo receivers can receive their cargo at destination. That is all for the cargo receivers' response with respect to GA.

After completion of GA Adjustment, the GA Adjusters will send the cargo insurers the GA Adjustment (GA Statement) together with their debit note for GA proportion of the cargo. Having scrutinised the contents of GA Adjustment and the cause of accident, the cargo underwriters will pay the GA proportion to the GA Adjusters. When the original GA Securities were returned to them, the activity of the cargo insurers in respect of this GA case terminates.

Well then, if the cargo is not insured, what will happen? In such a situation, the cargo receivers cannot submit the Average Guarantee signed by their cargo underwriters.

In place of Average Guarantee, the cargo receivers need to pay Cash Deposit requested by the shipowners or GA Adjusters (say, 20% of C&F Value). It is very troublesome for the cargo receivers to pay Cash Deposit in addition to the price of the imported cargo in order to receive their cargo at destination.

When the Cash Deposit is paid, the shipowners or GA Adjusters will issue General Average Deposit Receipt. Please keep it with caution since the cargo receivers may receive the balance between the Cash Deposit and their GA proportion in exchange for the original GA Deposit Receipt in due course. [8]

From the above, you will now understand when the cargo is not insured, the cargo owner may get involved in trouble and have to cope with the necessary procedures all by themselves.

---

(6) When the credit rating of the cargo underwriters is high, most of the shipowners and GA Adjusters will accept their signed Letter of Guarantee. If their credit rating is low, in lieu of their Letter of Guarantee, Bank Guarantee issued by high credit rating bank or Cash Deposit in US dollar to the shipowners or GA Adjusters may be requested. Please note that when the accident happens, the credibility of the cargo underwriters is essential and will present a problem.

(7) Having submitted GA Securities, if the cargo sustained damage, the cargo underwriters will notice the loss of and/or damage to their insured cargo, which is necessary for GA adjusters to calculate the net arrived value of the cargo for adjusting GA.

(8) In my practical experience as Average Adjuster, I collected GA Cash Deposit in the amount of US$50,000.00 on the second-hand vehicles exported to a Southeast Asian country. And I also found that household goods had been shipped abroad uninsured.

# Chapter 5

# What kind of expenses can be allowed in General Average?

In previous Chapters, I have explained general idea of General Average, what the cargo owners need to do when they receive a GA Declaration Letter, and how their cargo underwriters will cope with the situation, upon receipt of a notice from the cargo owners. In this Chapter I am explaining to you what kind of expenses can be allowed in GA.

As I said before, to constitute GA, it is essential that (1) the ship and the cargo were saved out from the common maritime peril and (2) they arrived at destination and the voyage ended.

With respect to (2) above, in exchange for receiving freight, the carriers are responsible for transporting the cargo to destination safely. When a casualty, such as stranding or collision, happens which give rise to a GA situation, the shipowners consider at first to put the ship into a port of refuge by her own power or under tow of salvage boat(s). Having secured safety there, necessary survey or repairs, which enable the ship to continue the voyage, will be conducted, and the cargo will then be transported to destination by the original vessel. This is the basic pattern of GA.

In line with this basic pattern, most of the extra expenditures to complete the voyage can be allowed in GA. In other words, when the ship transports the cargo to destination, usually the following expenses can be allowed in GA: [9]

① Salvage Remunerations

② Port charges and agency fees incurred by the ship's entry to and departure from the port of refuge (excluding the cost solely for her repairs)

③ The cost of temporarily discharging the cargo from the ship, storing and reloading them after the completion of the repairs (when temporary discharge of all or a part of the cargo is necessary to effect damage repairs)

④ Wages and maintenance of the crew during the extra prolongation of the voyage due to the ship's entry into a port of refuge, and the costs of bunkers and fresh

---

(9) Expenses allowed in GA are called as General Average Expenditures.

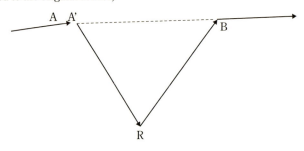

Extra prolongation of the voyage due to deviation to the port of refuge: A'R + RB - AB

A (Place of accident)
A' (Commenced moving to a port of refuge)
R (Entered the port of refuge)
B (Returned to the original course)

water consumed during this period.[10]

But quite often this basic pattern of GA does not take place. In reality, due to many other factors such as commercial decision by the shipowners, the actual course is very different from this basic pattern of GA.

Let's say, when it will take significant period of time to effect permanent repairs of the vessel at the port of refuge, in order to expedite transport of the cargo to destination, the following options can be taken:

① Having effected temporary repairs, the ship will continue the voyage to destination.

② Having transshipped all the cargo to other vessel(s), which called as 'the substituted vessel(s)', and which will carry the cargo to destination.

③ From the port of refuge, the ship and the cargo will be towed to destination.

Any additional expenses which are incurred by taking the above options; namely ① the cost of temporary repairs, ② the extra cost of forwarding the cargo by the substituted vessel, or ③ towing expense to destination, are allowed in GA. However, this allowance in GA is only up to the amount which would have been allowed in GA had the

---

(10) The extra prolongation of the voyage means that the extra time spent from the ship's move to the port of refuge to her returning to the original course less the estimated time which would have been taken from the point of the accident to the point of returning to the original course in a usual sea voyage, namely the extra time actually taken compared to when the accident had not happened.

Chapter 5   What kind of expenses can be allowed in General Average?

ship effected permanent repairs at the port of refuge or the nearest available repair port. Namely, this maximum allowable amount is the aggregate amount of the estimated GA expenditures; such as the cost of temporarily discharging, storing and reloading the cargo. In other words, the additional expenses incurred by taking the options can be allowed in GA only up to the estimated amount had the basic pattern of GA been adopted. This is called as 'substituted expenses'. From the estimated ordinary expenses which would have been incurred by the ship if the accident had not happened will be deducted

Since way of thinking, 'substituted expenses' is a very important concept for understanding GA system and what kind of expenditures can be allowed in GA, in Chapter 6, I shall show you an example for your better understanding.

# Chapter 6

# Specific example of the substituted expenses

Well, in this chapter, let's talk about substituted expenses. To fully understand the system of General Average, substituted expenses are a very important concept to consider what kind of expenditures and to what extent those expenditures can be allowed in GA. Now I will explain to you by showing a specific example for your better understanding.

Whilst the general cargo vessel "AAA" (17,999 gross tonnes), laden with 26,000 metric tonnes of steel products, was proceeding from Chiba, Japan to Los Angels, USA, she went aground off Tateyama, Japan. As a result of the grounding, she sustained extensive crack and dent damage to her bottom. Fortunately she could proceed with her own power, and put herself into Yokohama to take refuge which was the nearest available port to effect permanent repairs of the damage.

Having inspected the damage and consulted with the ship repair yard, it was found that to accomplish the voyage to Los Angeles it was necessary to temporarily discharge the whole cargo of 26,000 metric tonnes from the vessel at Yokohama, and to effect permanent repairs in a dry dock. Had she continued the voyage after completion of the permanent repairs, she must have been stayed there for two months.

Having completed the permanent repairs, had the vessel continued the voyage to Los Angeles, the following costs of temporarily discharging, storing and reloading the cargo totalling to JPY145,500,000 would have been allowed in general average (This is the basic pattern of general average):

Meanwhile, at the request of the cargo owners, the cargo was actually forwarded by the substituted vessel "SSS" to Los Angeles and the cost of forwarding all the cargo by the substituted vessel totalling to JPY148,500,000 were incurred as follows:

| | |
|---|---|
| Cost of temporarily discharging 26,000 MT of the steel products | JPY57,000,000 |
| Cost of storing 26,000 MT of the steel products for 2 months | JPY31,500,000 |
| Cost of reloading the temporarily discharged 26,000 MT of steel products onto the vessel | JPY57,000,000 |
| Total | JPY145,500,000 (A) |

# Chapter 6  Specific example of the substituted expenses

| Cost of temporarily discharging 26,000 MT of the steel products | JPY57,000,000 | |
|---|---|---|
| Cost of storing 26,000 MT of the steel products for 1 week | JPY3,500,000 | |
| Cost of loading the temporarily discharged 26,000 MT of steel products onto the substituted vessel | JPY57,000,000 | |
| Cost of hiring the substituted vessel "SSS" | JPY30,000,000 | |
| Port charges of the substituted vessel "SSS" at Los Angeles | JPY1,000,000 | |
| Total | JPY148,500,000 | (B) |

When the cargo was forwarded by the substituted vessel, since the vessel did not need to navigate from the point of the accident off Tateyama to Los Angeles, the following ordinary voyage expenses of the vessel totalling to JPY10,000,00 were saved:

| Wages and maintenance of the vessel's crew during the saved period | JPY6,000,000 | |
|---|---|---|
| Cost of bunkers and fresh water consumed during the saved period | JPY3,000,000 | |
| Port charges of the vessel "AAA" at Los Angeles | JPY1,000,000 | |
| Expected ordinary voyage expenses saved by the vessel | JPY10,000,000 | (C) |

The net forwarding charges by the substituted vessel in the amount of JPY138,500,000 (Gross forwarding charges JPY148,500,000 (B) above less expected ordinary voyage expenses saved by the vessel JPY10,000,000 (C) above) are allowed in general average as substituted expenses up to the basic pattern (A) above; (had the vessel effected permanent repairs at Yokohama, the cost of temporarily discharging, storing and reloading the cargo amounted to JPY145,500,000 (A)). In this example, the net forwarding charges by the substituted vessel in the amount of JPY138,500,000 are fully allowed in general average as substituted expenses.

On the other hand, if the net forwarding charges by the substituted vessel amount to JPY150,000,000, only JPY145,500,000 is allowed in general average as substituted expenses and the remaining JPY4,500,000 is not allowed in GA.

Although the above example seems to be a little complicated, I hope you will grasp the general idea which expenditures are allowed in GA, and how and to what extent the expenditures are allowed in GA as substituted expenses.

II   A Clear Guide to General Average

# Chapter 7

## What kind of losses can be allowed in General Average?

In Chapters 5 and 6 I have explained what kind of expenses can be allowed in General Average; especially, what kind of expenditures incurred to save the ship and the cargo from the common peril are allowed in GA, and the concept of substituted expenses.

In addition to such expenses payable to the third parties, the loss of the ship and/or the cargo as a result of the intentional general average act to save them from the common peril can also be allowed in GA. Well, in this chapter, let's see typical GA losses (sacrifices).

### 1   Damage done to the ship or the cargo by fire fighting operations

Fire is a typical accident to endanger the ship and the cargo in common peril. When the fire broke out, the ship or the cargo might sustain fire damage (burnt, smoke or heat damage), and to extinguish the fire, water might be poured into the ship's cargo hold (storing place of the cargo onboard the ship), and as a result, the ship or the cargo may sustain water damage.

Since burnt, smoke or heat damage is considered to be caused by an accidental incident; a fire, such fire damage is borne by the ship or the cargo. As the loss is borne by a particular interest, this is called Particular Average (PA). On the other hand, as a result of intentional act of extinguishing the fire, the ship and the cargo may sustain water or rust damage. Since these losses are the direct consequence of the general average act which was conducted deliberately to save the ship and the cargo, those losses are allowed in general average; which are called general average sacrifice.

By pouring water (general average act), further smoke or heat damage might happen, Rule III of York-Antwerp Rules 1994 clearly states that no compensation (as GA) shall be made for damage by smoke however caused or by heat of the fire.

In case fire fighting damage to the ship or the cargo is expected, it is very difficult to apportion (direct) fire damage and water damage. As far as there is a time to despatch GA surveyor for general interest, to avoid the possible future dispute, normally GA adjuster, the shipowners or the hull & machinery underwriters appoint GA surveyor who will attend the ship for the general interest to ascertain and apportion the fire damage and water damage (fire fighting damage). It is very important to conduct GA survey by jointly attending with surveyors representing the ship and/or the cargo interests so that the ascertainment (approval) of the fire and water damage will not be different among the surveyors.

### 2  Damage done to the ship or the cargo as a result of salvage operations

Damage done to the ship or the cargo as a result of the salvage operations to save the ship and the cargo from the common peril is also allowed as general average sacrifice.

Let me show you a specific example.

For example, when a ship went aground, if a part of the cargo was temporarily discharged onto the barge to refloat the ship and, after refloating, the temporarily discharged cargo was reloaded onto the ship, the damage done to the ship or the cargo by temporarily discharging and reloading the cargo is allowed in general average.

And when the cargo was thrown out from the ship (jettisoned) to refloat the grounded ship, the damage done to the cargo is allowed as general average sacrifice. But at present throwing out of the dangerous or toxic substance into the sea are strictly prohibited by law, it is very rare to throw out (jettison) the cargo to save the ship and the cargo.

Although damage due to the grounding is allowed as particular average under the hull & machinery policy, damage done to ship by refloating operation as a general average act, and damage done to the ship's engine by extra use to refloat the grounded ship in peril are allowed as general average sacrifice.

In such a case it is necessary for GA surveyor to approve the extent and costs of the ship's damage due to refloating or salvage operations. In theory, the ship's damage due to grounding is particular average under the hull & machinery insurance policy and the damage done to the ship due to refloating operation is general average sacrifice, since it is very difficult to ascertain and distinguish the ship's grounding and refloating damages, in practice among the average adjusters, it is very rare that the refloating damage of the ship is allowed as general average sacrifice.

As above, the theory of general average and the current practice of general average are sometimes different. However, it is good to know the theory in order to understand the core principle of general average.

## 3  Loss of the ship or the cargo as a result of cargo handling at the port of refuge

Loss of the ship and/or the cargo due to temporarily discharging, reloading the cargo to effect the ship's repairs which were necessary to accomplish the intended voyage, and due to transshipping the cargo onto the substituted vessel are also allowed as general average sacrifice.

Especially with respect to bulk cargo such as crude oil, chemical products, grains, etc., cargo handlings will inevitably cause shortage of the cargo. Extra shortage of the bulk cargo exceeding the ordinary shortage in a usual voyage had the accident not happened is allowed as general average sacrifice.

## 4  Loss of the ship or the cargo by re-stowing the cargo for the common safety

From now on, I will tell you a memorable case which I as an average adjuster together with a GA surveyor, had attended the disabled ship under salvage at the port of refuge.

A cargo ship, laden with steel coils encountered heavy weather during the voyage. As a result, the cargo was shifted in the cargo holds, and the ship was listed to 40 degrees to her starboard side, and became a very dangerous situation of overturning and sinking. All the ship crewmembers abandoned the ship, and the ship with no crew had continued to be drifting, and faced a risk of grounding near shallow place.

The shipowners requested the salvors to save the ship and the cargo, and she was managed to be towed into a port of refuge by a powerful salvage tugboat although she was still in unstable listed conditions in the port. Usually when the ship was put into a port of refuge, so far as she was stayed in the port, she became physically safety. But, in this particular case, even when the ship was put into the port of refuge, she still listed 20 degrees to her starboard side, and was still in a peril of overturning and sinking, and the salvage operations were continued until regaining stability of the ship.

At the request of the shipowners and the hull & machinery underwriters, I as an average adjuster together with a GA surveyor, attended the ship under salvage which was berthed at the port of refuge, and consulted with the salvage master who commanded the salvage operations. The ship list in 20 degrees was really steep, and I felt a real danger.

Under the circumstances, to restore the stability of the ship, it was decided that until

## Chapter 7  What kind of losses can be allowed in General Average?

restoring her stability, the cargo was temporarily discharged by using a shore crane, and stored in open yard.

When the cargo is temporarily discharged and/or re-stowed to secure the common safety of the ship and the cargo as above, the loss of the ship and/or the cargo due to temporarily discharging, re-stowing, handling and reloading the cargo are allowed in general average.

From these four examples, you will understand what kind of losses can be allowed in general average.

# Chapter 8

# What are York-Antwerp Rules?

In Chapter 1, I explained to you General Average is a natural law of the sea which was borne nearly 3,000 years ago. At present York-Antwerp Rules (hereinafter called YAR) is the basis of adjusting General Average. In this chapter I would like to explain to you what YAR are.

Well, there are four things I would like you to know about YAR.

At first, are YAR a convention or law? Secondly, why are the shipowners and the cargo owners bound to YAR? Thirdly, how have YAR been amended? Lastly, how are YAR composed of?

## 1  Are YAR a convention or law?

I tell you a conclusion at the beginning, YAR are not a convention or law in a particular nation. By listening to opinions of the various interests involved in carriage by sea, international association of maritime law experts called Comite Maritime International (CMI) have been adopted and reviewed YAR. Although YAR are international uniform rules, which are not a convention or law. There are several versions of YAR such as YAR 1974, YAR 1994, YAR 2004 and YAR 2016. This point will be explained in some detail later on.

## 2  Why are the shipowners and the cargo owners bound to YAR?

Although YAR are international uniform rules, they are not naturally applied to the parties involved in a voyage. Well then, why are the shipowners and the cargo owners bound to YAR, which are not a convention or law. The reason is, in the first instance, the shipowners states in the contract of carriage by sea that when a General Average situation arises, GA shall be adjusted according to YAR. Once the cargo owners have agreed to them, YAR have become a part of the contract of carriage by sea.

To understand the above point, let us look at some history. With respect to General

Average, whilst England traditionally relied on the concept of the common safety (when the ship enters a port of refuge and becomes safety conditions, General Average terminates), nations in European Continent such as France relied on the concept of completion of the intended voyage (when the scheduled voyage terminates, General Average ends).

When there is a difference in nationalities between the shipowners and the cargo owners, and if the concept (extent) of General Average differs among those nations, you can imagine there will be serious practical problems in adjusting General Average.

To uniform the treatment of each nation's General Average, in 1860 Glasgow Resolutions were adopted, in 1864 York Rules and, then, in 1877 York-Antwerp Rules were adopted. After a very long discussion and arguments, finally, some 140 years ago YAR was formed.

At the very beginning of this lengthy process, the parties concerned with maritime law had thought that it would be desirable to enact "uniform General Average law", and had been tried to do so for many years. But this was met with conflicts among various complicated interests, and it was shared among the parties that it was very hard to enact the uniform GA law. To overcome these difficulties, they set the next goal; "voluntary uniform of General Average Rules", namely, by adopting uniform GA Rules and insert these Rules into contracts of carriage by sea between the shipowners and the cargo owners. By this way of efforts made by the parties concerned, at present, in almost every contract of carriage by sea YAR are inserted and agreed among the parties concerned.

### 3  How have YAR been amended?

Although it took many years to uniform General Average Rules; YAR, it is not saying that YAR are unchanged forever. Reflecting on change from the age of sail ships to the age of steel motor vessels, and on requests of each time, YAR have been amended in 1890, 1924, 1950, 1974, 1990, 1994, 2004 and 2016.

With respect to YAR, at present, having been listening to the parties concerned such as the shipowners and the cargo owners, each national maritime law association and average adjusters, etc., Comite Maritime International (CMI), which was headquartered at Antwerp, Belgium has been reviewing and adopting the revised new Rules. YAR have original texts in English and French. YAR 2016 have original text in English only.

## 4  How are YAR composed of ?

Since YAR 1994 are presently the most adopted in contracts of carriage by sea, I will explain the compositions of YAR1994.

YAR1994 consist of the following four parts:

① Rule of Interpretation: This rule states that how you should construe YAR.

② Rule Paramount: This rule provides a very important discipline that only reasonable sacrifice or expenditure can be allowed in GA.

③ Lettered Rules: From Rule A to Rule G

④ Numbered Rules: From Rule I to Rule XXII

Lettered Rules provides the general principles of GA, and numbered Rules states in which concrete situation the expenditures and/or sacrifices can be allowed in GA, and how these will be apportioned among the ship, the bunkers and the cargo, etc.

Since Rule of Interpretation provides that except as provided by the Rule Paramount and the numbered Rules, GA shall be adjusted according to the lettered Rules, the numbered Rules precede the lettered Rules.

# Chapter 9

# Major points of difference between YAR 1994 and YAR 2016

In Chapter 8, I explained to you what York-Antwerp Rules (hereinafter called YAR) are.

Whilst YAR 1994 are presently the most adopted in the contracts of carriage by sea such as bills of lading and charter parties, a new version of YAR; YAR 2016 has been adopted at CMI conference held in New York City in May 2016.

There are three major points of difference between YAR 1994 and YAR 2016 as follows:

① Whether or not salvage remuneration will be allowed in general average
② Commission and interest on general average disbursements
③ Time bar for contributions to general average

I would like to explain to you about three points one by one.

## 1  Whether or not salvage remuneration will be allowed in GA

There are three types of salvage contract to salve (save) the ship and the cargo.

The first type is Lumpsum contract, in which the salvors and the shipowners have agreed the whole amount of salvage remuneration at the time of signing the salvage contract.

The second type is Daily Hire contract, in which the salvors and the shipowners have agreed the daily amount of salvage remuneration at the time of signing the salvage contract.

The third type is LOF (Lloyd's Standard Form of Salvage Agreement) or JSE Form (Japan Shipping Exchange Form). Under these contracts, salvage remuneration is not agreed at the time of signing the salvage contract, and the salvage remuneration will be decided by taking into consideration of the values of the salved properties and difficulty of the salvage operations, etc. after termination of the salvage operations.

To help your easy understanding, I prepare Table 1. Whether or not salvage remuneration will be allowed in GA as below.

Under Rule VI of YAR 1994, salvage remunerations incurred, to salve the ship and the cargo from the common peril, are allowed in GA under all types of salvage contracts.

Under Rule VI of YAR 2016, however, whilst the salvage remunerations under Lumpsum or Daily Hire contracts are allowed in GA, the salvage remunerations under LOF or JSE form will not be allowed in GA unless any of the situations stated in Table 1 arises such as (i) there is a subsequent accident or other circumstances resulting in loss or damage to property during the voyage that results in significant differences between salved and contributory values.

In adjusting GA under YAR 2016, average adjusters need to decide whether or not there were significant differences on each case. This is considered to be a big change in the adjuster's world.

Although, in theory, the salvage remunerations under all types of salvage contracts incurred to salve the ship and the cargo from the common danger are allowed in GA under Rule A of YAR, to achieve early settlement and to reduce time for adjusting general average, as a compromise among the parties involved in the common maritime adventure, Rule VI of YAR 2016 states in this way. As a result, LOF salvage remunerations will not be allowed in GA in most cases.

Table 1  Whether or not salvage remuneration will be allowed in GA

| Salvage Contract | Salvage requestor | Who are liable to pay salvage remuneration | under YAR 1994 | under YAR 2016 |
|---|---|---|---|---|
| Lumpsum or Daily Hire Contract | Shipowner | The shipowner is legally liable to pay whole salvage remuneration to a salvor. | Allowed in GA | Allowed in GA |
| LOF (Lloyd's Standard Form of Salvage Agreement) or JSE Form (Japan Shipping Exchange Form) | Captain or Shipowner | Each owner of the salved property; such as the ship and the cargo, etc. is independently and separately legally liable to pay respective proportion of the salvage remuneration. | Allowed in GA | Basically, not allowed in GA. But, allowed in GA should any of the following arise:<br>(i)  there is a subsequent accident or other circumstances resulting in loss or damage to property during the voyage that results in significant differences between salved and contributory values,<br>(ii)  there are significant |

# Chapter 9  Major points of difference between YAR 1994 and YAR 2016

| | | | | | general average sacrifices, (iii) salved values are manifestly incorrect and there is a significant incorrect apportionment of salvage expenses, (iv) any of the parties to the salvage has paid a significant proportion of salvage due from another party, (v) a significant proportion of the parties have satisfied the salvage claim on substantially different terms, no regard being had to interest, currency correction or legal costs of either the salvor or the contributing interest. |
|---|---|---|---|---|---|

## 2  Commission and interest on general average disbursements

Under YAR 2016 a commission of 2 % on general average disbursements has been abolished, and interest rate has been changed to floating rate based on 12-month ICE LIBOR for the currency used in the adjustment. For more details, please see Table 2.

## 3  Time bar for contributions to general average

The third point is time bar for contributions to general average. Since there was no provision on time bar under YAR 1994, the time bar will be determined according to the governing law under the contract of carriage. When the governing law is English law and GA securities have been obtained from the cargo interests, it is construed that, under the Limitation Act 1980, the time bar for contributions to general average is 6 years after an issuance of GA Adjustment. When Japanese law is applied, under Commercial Code Article 812 (ex Article 798), the time bar is 1 year after an issuance of GA Adjustment.

Under YAR 2016 any rights to general average contribution shall be extinguished unless an action is brought by the party claiming such contribution within 1 year after the GA Adjustment is issued. However, in no case shall such an action be brought after 6 years from the end of the voyage.

When the GA accident happened on a container ship, it may easily take more than 5 years to issue a GA Adjustment, and may take more than 2 years to collect GA contributions from thousands of the cargo interests. When YAR 2016 is applied without change, we shall face the problem of the time bar for contributions to general average.

## 4 Outlook

It took more than 10 years to change applicable rules under the contract of carriage from YAR 1974 to YAR 1994. In the same way, it may take more than 10 years for YAR 1994 and YAR 2016 to be concurrently adopted in various contracts of carriage.

Even when YAR 2016 become applicable, until the whole salvage remunerations under LOF (Lloyd's Open Form) or JSE Form (Japan Shipping Exchange Form) have been determined, GA Adjustment cannot be completed just as in the present situation under YAR 1994.

Table 2  Commission and interest on general average disbursements

|  | YAR | under YAR 1994 | under YAR 2016 |
|---|---|---|---|
| Commission | Rule XX | A commission of 2 % on general average disbursements shall be allowed in GA. | Abolished. |
| Interest | Rule XXI | Interest shall be allowed on expenditure, sacrifices and allowances in GA at the rate of 7 % per annum, until three months after the date of issue of the GA adjustment. | Interest shall be allowed on expenditure, sacrifices and allowances in GA until three months after the date of issue of the GA adjustment. The rate for calculating interest accruing during each calendar year shall be the 12-month ICE LIBOR* for the currency in which the adjustment is prepared, as announced on the first banking day of that calendar year, increased by four percentage points. |
|  |  |  | Applicable rates during 2017 for each currency are as follows:<br>USD 5.689% per annum<br>JPY 4.12771% per annum<br>EUR 3.91357% per annum |

\* Note: ICE LIBOR stands for Intercontinental Exchange London Interbank Offered Rates, which is the average of the interest rates that some of the world banks charges each other for short-term loans.

## Chapter 9  Major points of difference between YAR 1994 and YAR 2016

Lastly, since the time bar for contributions to general average will be shorter compared to under YAR 1994, we may face problem of the time bar in day-to-day practice. Since CMI have noticed the problem, they will discuss and act to eliminate this problem in the near future.

# Chapter 10

# The job and the roles of GA adjusters

In this chapter I will explain to you the job and the roles of GA adjusters.

## 1   Self-introduction as a GA adjuster

In Chapter 1, I wrote, such as a one-time best-seller 'If the world were a village of 100 people', only about 100 active GA adjusters in the world are currently preparing formal Adjustment of General Average, and I am one of three GA adjusters in Japan.

More than 35 years ago in my sophomore year at a university, I was interested in learning cultures of foreign countries and international trade. With an introduction from a senior student at my English club, I happened to have joined a marine insurance seminar. When I graduated from the university, following recommendation from my seminar professor, I decided to join an average adjusting office. After seven-year training of adjusting GA in Tokyo, I studied actual average adjusting cases under guidance of prominent average adjusters for one year at two major average adjusting offices in London and New York. After returning to Tokyo, I had assisted in preparing adjustments. Then, I have become preparing GA adjustments by myself as a GA adjuster.

## 2   Practical experience is essential to become a GA adjuster

Suppose you intend to become a GA adjuster, even though you started to prepare adjustments by yourself, or even though you have business cards which clearly introduce you as a GA adjuster, you cannot continue to work as a GA adjuster if your GA adjustments are not accepted by the ship, the cargo and the other parties concerned. Even if you fully memorise the text of the York-Antwerp Rules, since YAR only state the general principles and judgment standard, by applying the relevant YAR to each case, it is necessary for you to make judgments in fair and impartial way to all the parties concerned. To apply YAR to each case, naturally, it is essential to consider the rules and

Chapter 10  The job and the roles of GA adjusters

practice in shipping and ocean trade, and to refer to the common sense in our society.

I often recall my mentor, late Mr Jim O'Shea, during training average adjusting at a major average adjusting office in the City of London. He was always saying to me that, to become a good average adjuster, you should read thoroughly maritime newspapers such as Lloyd's List together with major national newspapers. Through my practical experience I believe that his words are true and correct. As a GA adjuster, to decide what should be allowed in GA and what not, and to convince all the parties concerned to settle their GA proportions, it is very important to have common sense in a shipping world and as an ordinary citizen. The more you have practical experiences and opportunities to review many cases, the more opportunities to assist very difficult adjusting cases and to think together with your senior adjusters and, to read adjustments after issuance, I am sure that your ability as a GA adjuster will be much improved.

### 3  Let's look at the job and roles of GA adjusters

The most important job of GA adjusters is, under the applicable YAR stated in the contract of carriage; such as bill of lading or charter party, to make a fair decision and prepare GA adjustments, which state that how much the actual expenses or losses incurred to cope with the ship's accident are allowed in GA, and how much each party concerned such as the ship, the cargo and the others should finally contribute GA. It is correctly said that the job of GA adjusters is just like a fair and impartial judge or an accountant.

The job of GA adjusters is originally to prepare GA adjustments. In exchange for issuance of a GA adjustment, the adjusters received their adjusting fees from the client, and completed their job. Originally, based on the GA adjustment, the shipowners by themselves or through their agents, insurance brokers sent debit notes to the hull & machinery and the cargo underwriters, and collected GA proportions from them.

But from 1970s in addition to preparing GA adjustments, English GA adjusters commenced collecting GA proportions from each party (settlement of GA) on behalf of the shipowners. Gradually, at the request of the shipowners, GA adjusters in other countries also started collection of GA proportions. In this way, currently the job of GA adjusters expands up to the settlements of GA from the preparation of GA adjustments.

And the scope of job of GA adjusters depends upon each nation. In the UK, Europe, the USA, Singapore and Hong Kong, etc. the shipowners or their agents, insurance brokers usually appoint average adjusters to prepare PA adjustments (adjustments of particular average such as the cost of damage repairs and particular charges) in addition to GA adjustments. On the other hand, in Japan, since the assessment of the ship's PA amounts payable under the hull & machinery policy has been traditionally conducted by the hull & machinery underwriters without appointing average adjusters to prepare PA adjustments, the main job of average adjusters in Japan is preparation of GA adjustments.

Furthermore, except GA cases when there is a dispute on allocation of the extra expenses among the ship and the cargo interests, it is often seen in every country to ask for an average adjusters' impartial opinion, since the adjusters are very familiar with GA and the other maritime law and contracts, and the hull & machinery and cargo insurances, and are also very good at adjusting difference of opinions and difficulties among the parties concerned.

### 4  Let's look at what GA adjusters will do along with the developments of the ship's accident

When the shipowners decide to ask the cargo, the bunkers and the container interests to contribute General Average, which is called formal General Average, the shipowners usually appoint GA adjusters and declare General Average, and obtain GA securities form those interests.

The jobs of GA adjusters start at the very early stage of the accident by consulting and advising the shipowners and the hull & machinery underwriters the necessary steps to be taken, and preparing GA declaration; obtaining GA securities from the cargo interests, such as the consignees and the cargo underwriters before delivery of the cargo; issuing GA Adjustment; and finally end by completing the settlement of GA among the parties concerned.

Well then, let's look at what GA adjusters will do in more details step by step.

(1) GA Declaration and appointment of GA adjusters

When the ship laden with the cargo involved in a major accident, such as collision, stranding, fire, main engine breakdown, the ship list by the collapse of the cargo due to heavy weather, etc. during the voyage, and extensive amount of money is expected to be spent to save both the ship and the cargo, the shipowners decide to treat the case as formal General Average and to declare to the cargo in order to ask for contribution to

GA (GA Declaration), which will be informed to the consignees through the charterers or the shipowners' agents at destination. In GA Declaration the shipowners ask for submission of GA securities prior to receiving the cargo at destination, and appoint GA adjusters.

(2)　Appointment of GA Surveyors

When at the port of refuge the cargo handling (discharging, storing and reloading the cargo to effect permanent repairs of the ship, or transshipping the cargo onto the substituted vessel) is necessary, the shipowners, the hull & machinery underwriters or GA adjusters will appoint GA Surveyors (or General Interest Surveyors) to ascertain the sacrificial GA loss to the cargo due to the cargo handling.

When the cargo handling is not conducted at the port of refuge, or it is not expected the ship and/or the cargo GA sacrifice by fire extinguishing water, usually GA survey is not essential.

It is the duty and responsibility of GA Surveyors to ascertain the cargo damage due to the cargo handling at the port of refuge, and to advise the shipowners to make the cost of handling cargo as reasonable amount.

(3)　Application for Average Disbursements Insurance

Once the originally intended voyage ended, the ship and the cargo were saved by the general average act, and the duty to contribute to GA was established at the end of the voyage. In other words, in case the ship was sunk whilst the ship's departure from the port of refuge to arrival at destination, and became a total loss by the other accident, GA Disbursements advanced by the shipowners cannot be recoverable as GA from the hull & machinery underwriters and the cargo interests.

In order to prepare for such an unfortunate case, Average Disbursements Insurance covers the loss caused by the unrecoverable GA Disbursements already paid when the ship became a total loss by the other accident. To hedge the risk following advice from GA adjusters, the shipowners apply for Average Disbursements Insurance to their hull & machinery underwriters.

Although in the first instance the shipowners need to pay premium of Average Disbursements Insurance to the hull & machinery underwriters, the insurance premium can be allowed in general average, eventually the shipowners can recover the premium as their GA Disbursement from the hull & machinery and the cargo underwriters, etc.

Ⅱ   A Clear Guide to General Average

(4)   Collection of GA Securities from the cargo receivers

Prior to delivery of the cargo to the cargo receivers at destination, GA adjusters will obtain GA Securities form the cargo interests by appointing the shipowners' agents at discharge port, if necessary.

As I already explained to you in Chapter 3, GA Securities which need to be obtained from the cargo interests are as follows:

① Average Bond to be signed by the cargo receivers
② Average Guarantee to be signed by the cargo underwriters
③ Valuation Form to be signed by the cargo receivers
④ Commercial Invoice copy of the cargo

Until receipt of GA Securities from the cargo receivers, the shipowners have legal right not to deliver the cargo and can hold the cargo in their custody. But once the cargo has been delivered, which means the shipowners' right to hold the cargo has been lapsed, the shipowners will lose their legal ground for requesting GA Securities from the cargo interests. As a result, it is essential for the shipowners to obtain GA Securities before delivery of the cargo at destination.

(5)   The relevant parties submit the necessary documents to GA adjusters

About the time when the necessary steps to save both the ship and the cargo are being completed, GA adjusters will advise the relevant parties, namely, the shipowners, the hull & machinery and the cargo underwriters, the list of the necessary documents to be submitted for adjusting general average, and each of those relevant parties send GA adjusters already obtained documents hop-by-hop. Since GA commission at 2 % and GA interest per annum at 7 % on GA Disbursements (from the date of payment until three months after the date of issue of the GA Adjustment) shall be allowed in GA under York-Antwerp Rules 1994, the parties need to inform the respective date of their payments to GA adjusters. GA adjusters calculate GA commission and interest on each item of GA Disbursements.

(6)   Issuance of GA Adjustment

Based on the documents submitted by the shipowners, the hull & machinery and the cargo underwriters, GA adjusters will prepare and issue GA Adjustment which shows the GA allowances out of Disbursements and/or Sacrificial Loss sustained as a result of GA Act, and the GA proportions of the ship and the cargo, etc.

## Chapter 10  The job and the roles of GA adjusters

(7)  Settlement of General Average

When GA adjusters are instructed not only to adjust GA but also to settle the GA, in other words, to collect the GA proportions and to apportion among the parties, GA adjusters ask the hull & machinery and cargo underwriters, etc., to pay their GA proportions to their bank account. Upon completion of recovery from the parties concerned, by paying each amount of Disbursements to be received, Settlement of General Average by the average adjusters ends.

### 5  GA adjusters' thought

In long time experience of adjusting General Averages, GA adjusters might face very difficult GA cases which even though the drafters of York-Antwerp Rules had not anticipated.

In such cases, having reviewed the documents submitted and having grasped a rough outline of the complicated circumstances, to find a solution among the parties concerned, GA adjusters sometimes take a step to visit the shipowners' office and to listen to the very dangerous situation of the ship and the cargo from the superintendent who attended the scene of the accident. After that, based on the facts and collected information, under the applicable York-Antwerp Rules, GA adjusters prepare a draft Adjustment which will be acceptable to the ship and the cargo interests, and explain the contents to all the parties. Having obtained agreement, GA adjusters try to adjust and settle GA as soon as possible.

As a GA adjuster I shall continue to adjust each case in the balanced mind for all the parties involved in the common maritime adventure.

# III

## 1994年ヨーク・アントワープ規則対訳集
## York-Antwerp Rules 1994
(1999年7月東京マリンクレームサービス株式会社発行)

## York-Antwerp Rules 1994

### RULE OF INTERPRETATION

In the adjustment of general average **the following Rules** shall apply to the exclusion of any Law and Practice inconsistent therewith.

Except as provided by **the Rule Paramount and** the numbered Rules, general average shall be adjusted according to the lettered Rules.

### RULE PARAMOUNT
**In no case shall there be any allowance for sacrifice or expenditure unless reasonably made or incurred.**

### Rule A
There is a general average act when, and only when, any extraordinary sacrifice or expenditure is intentionally and reasonably made or incurred for the common safety for the purpose of preserving from peril the property involved in a common maritime adventure.

General average sacrifices and **expenditures** shall be borne by the different contributing interests on the basis hereinafter provided.

## York-Antwerp Rules 1974 as amended 1990

### RULE OF INTERPRETATION

In the adjustment of general average the following lettered and numbered Rules shall apply to the exclusion of any Law and Practice inconsistent therewith.

Except as provided by the numbered Rules, general average shall be adjusted according to the lettered Rules.

### Rule A
There is a general average act when, and only when, any extraordinary sacrifice or expenditure is intentionally and reasonably made or incurred for the common safety for the purpose of preserving from peril the property involved in a common maritime adventure.

### Rule B
General average sacrifices and expenses shall be borne by the different contributing interests on the basis hereinafter provided.

解釈規定

| 1994年ヨーク・アントワープ規則 | 1990年修正<br>1974年ヨーク・アントワープ規則 |
|---|---|
| 解釈規定<br>　共同海損の精算にあたっては、次の諸規定を、これらと矛盾する一切の法律および慣習を排除して適用する。<br><br>　至上規定および数字規定により規定された場合を除き、共同海損は文字規定に従い精算する。<br><br>至上規定<br>　いかなる場合にも、犠牲または費用は、合理的になされるか、または支出されたものでなければ認容してはならない。<br><br>A条<br>　共同の航海団体を構成する財産を危険から守る意図をもって、共同の安全のために、故意にかつ合理的に、異常の犠牲を払い、または費用を支出した場合に限り、共同海損行為が成立する。<br><br>　共同海損となる犠牲および費用は、以下に規定するところに基づいて、各種の分担利益が負担する。 | 解釈規定<br>　共同海損の精算にあたっては、次の文字規定および数字規定を、これらと矛盾する一切の法律および慣習を排除して適用する。<br><br>　数字規定により規定された場合を除き、共同海損は文字規定に従い精算する。<br><br><br><br>A条<br>　共同の航海団体を構成する財産を危険から守る意図をもって、共同の安全のために、故意にかつ合理的に、異常の犠牲を払い、または費用を支出した場合に限り、共同海損行為が成立する。<br><br>B条<br>　共同海損となる犠牲および費用は、以下に規定するところに基づいて、各種の分担利益が負担する。 |

| York-Antwerp Rules 1994 | York-Antwerp Rules 1974 as amended 1990 |
|---|---|

Rule B

**There is a common maritime adventure when one or more vessels are towing or pushing another vessel or vessels, provided that they are all involved in commercial activities and not in a salvage operation.**

**When measures are taken to preserve the vessels and their cargoes, if any, from a common peril, these Rules shall apply.**

**A vessel is not in common peril with another vessel or vessels if by simply disconnecting from the other vessel or vessels she is in safety; but if the disconnection is itself a general average act the common maritime adventure continues.**

Rule C

Only such losses, damages or expenses which are the direct consequence of the general average act shall be allowed as general average.

**In no case shall there be any allowance in general average for losses, damages or expenses incurred in respect of damage to the environment or in consequence of the escape or release of pollutant substances from the property involved in the common maritime adventure.**

Rule C

Only such losses, damages or expenses which are the direct consequence of the general average act shall be allowed as general average.

| 1994年ヨーク・アントワープ規則 | 1990年修正<br>1974年ヨーク・アントワープ規則 |

B条

　1隻または複数の船舶が他の1隻または複数の船舶を曳航しているか押航している場合は、共同の航海団体が存在する。ただし、それらの船舶すべてが商業活動に従事している場合であって、かつ、救助作業に従事していない場合に限る。

　かかる船舶、および積荷があればその積荷を、共同の危険から守るために措置が講じられた場合には、本規則を適用する。

　船舶が他の1隻または複数の船舶と単に切り離すことによって安全となる場合は、かかる船舶と他の1隻または複数の船舶とには共同の危険はない。ただし、その切り離し自体が共同海損行為である場合は、共同の航海団体が継続する。

| C条 | C条 |
| --- | --- |
| 　共同海損行為の直接の結果である滅失、損傷または費用に限り、共同海損として認容する。 | 　共同海損行為の直接の結果である滅失、損傷または費用に限り、共同海損として認容する。 |

　いかなる場合にも、共同の航海団体を構成する財産から生じた、環境損害に関する、または汚染物質の流出もしくは排出の結果としての滅失、損傷または費用は、共同海損として認容しない。

| York-Antwerp Rules 1994 | York-Antwerp Rules 1974 as amended 1990 |
|---|---|
| **Demurrage, loss of market, and any loss or damage sustained or expense incurred by reason of delay, whether on the voyage or subsequently, and any indirect loss whatsoever,** shall not be admitted as general average. | Loss or damage sustained by the ship or cargo through delay, whether on the voyage or subsequently, such as demurrage, and any indirect loss whatsoever, such as loss of market, shall not be admitted as general average. |
| Rule D | Rule D |
| Rights to contribution in general average shall not be affected, though the event which gave rise to the sacrifice or expenditure may have been due to the fault of one of the parties to the adventure, but this shall not prejudice any remedies or defences which may be open against or to that party in respect of such fault. | Rights to contribution in general average shall not be affected, though the event which gave rise to the sacrifice or expenditure may have been due to the fault of one of the parties to the adventure, but this shall not prejudice any remedies or defences which may be open against or to that party in respect of such fault. |
| Rule E | Rule E |
| The onus of proof is upon the party claiming in general average to show that the loss or expense claimed is properly allowable as general average. | The onus of proof is upon the party claiming in general average to show that the loss or expense claimed is properly allowable as general average. |
| **All parties claiming in general average shall give notice in writing to the average adjuster of the loss or expense in respect of which they claim contribution within 12 months of the date of the termination of the common maritime adventure.** | |

| 1994年ヨーク・アントワープ規則 | 1990年修正<br>1974年ヨーク・アントワープ規則 |
|---|---|
| 　航海中であるとまたは航海終了であるとを問わず、滞船料、商機の逸失および遅延によって被った一切の滅失もしくは損傷、またはそれによって生じた費用、ならびに一切の間接損害は、共同海損として認容しない。 | 　航海中であるとまたは航海終了であるとを問わず、滞船料のごとき遅延に基づいて船舶または積荷が被った滅失もしくは損傷、または商機の逸失のごとき一切の間接損害は、共同海損として認容しない。 |
| D条<br>　犠牲または費用を生ぜしめた事故が航海団体の当事者のうちの一人の過失に起因した場合でも、共同海損の分担請求権は影響を受けない。ただし、この場合その当事者に対しかかる過失に関し求償または抗弁することを妨げない。 | D条<br>　犠牲または費用を生ぜしめた事故が航海団体の当事者のうちの一人の過失に起因した場合でも、共同海損の分担請求権は影響を受けない。ただし、この場合その当事者に対しかかる過失に関し求償または抗弁することを妨げない。 |
| E条<br>　共同海損への認容を請求する当事者は、その損失または費用が適法に共同海損として認容されることを立証する責めを負う。<br><br>　共同海損への認容を請求するすべての当事者は、分担を請求する損失または費用について、共同の航海団体終了の日から12か月以内に海損精算人に対して書面で通知しなければならない。 | E条<br>　共同海損への認容を請求する当事者は、その損失または費用が適法に共同海損として認容されることを立証する責めを負う。 |

| York-Antwerp Rules 1994 | York-Antwerp Rules 1974 as amended 1990 |
|---|---|

**Failing such notification, or if within 12 months of a request for the same any of the parties shall fail to supply evidence in support of a notified claim, or particulars of value in respect of a contributory interest, the average adjuster shall be at liberty to estimate the extent of the allowance or the contributory value on the basis of the information available to him, which estimate may be challenged only on the ground that it is manifestly incorrect.**

Rule F

Any **additional** expense incurred in place of another expense which would have been allowable as general average shall be deemed to be general average and so allowed without regard to the saving, if any, to other interests, but only up to the amount of the general average expense avoided.

Rule G

General average shall be adjusted as regards both loss and contribution upon the basis of values at the time and place when and where the adventure ends.

Rule F

Any extra expense incurred in place of another expense which would have been allowable as general average shall be deemed to be general average and so allowed without regard to the saving, if any, to other interests, but only up to the amount of the general average expense avoided.

Rule G

General average shall be adjusted as regards both loss and contribution upon the basis of values at the time and place when and where the adventure ends.

| 1994年ヨーク・アントワープ規則 | 1990年修正<br>1974年ヨーク・アントワープ規則 |

かかる通知がなされなかった場合、または通知した請求を証明する証拠、もしくは分担利益の価額の明細を求められてから12か月以内に当事者がこれを提出しなかった場合には、海損精算人は、入手しうる情報に基づいて認容の範囲または負担価額を見積ることができ、その見積りは明白に誤りであるという理由がある場合にのみ争うことができる。

F条
共同海損として認容されるべき他の費用の代わりに支出した追加の費用は、共同海損とみなし、共同海損以外の利益につき節約がなされたとしてもこれを考慮することなく、支出を免れた共同海損費用の金額の範囲内で共同海損に認容する。

F条
共同海損として認容されるべき他の費用の代わりに支出した余分の費用は、共同海損とみなし、共同海損以外の利益につき節約がなされたとしてもこれを考慮することなく、支出を免れた共同海損費用の金額の範囲内で共同海損に認容する。

G条
共同海損は、損失および分担額に関しては、航海終了の時および地における価額に基づいて精算する。

G条
共同海損は、損失および分担額に関しては、航海終了の時および地における価額に基づいて精算する。

York-Antwerp Rules 1994

This rule shall not affect the determination of the place at which the average statement is to be made up.

**When a ship is at any port or place in circumstances which would give rise to an allowance in general average under the provisions of Rules X and XI, and the cargo or part thereof is forwarded to destination by other means, rights and liabilities in general average shall, subject to cargo interests being notified if practicable, remain as nearly as possible the same as they would have been in the absence of such forwarding, as if the adventure had continued in the original ship for so long as justifiable under the contract of affreightment and the applicable law.**

**The proportion attaching to cargo of the allowances made in general average by reason of applying the third paragraph of this Rule shall not exceed the cost which would have been borne by the owners of cargo if the cargo had been forwarded at their expense.**

York-Antwerp Rules 1974
as amended 1990

This rule shall not affect the determination of the place at which the average statement is to be made up.

## G条

| 1994年ヨーク・アントワープ規則 | 1990年修正<br>1974年ヨーク・アントワープ規則 |
| --- | --- |
| 本条は、共同海損精算書の作成されるべき地を取り決めたものではない。 | 本条は、共同海損精算書の作成されるべき地を取り決めたものではない。 |
| 船舶がある港または地にある場合で、X条およびXI条の規定によって共同海損の認容を生ぜしめるような状況の下で、積荷の全部または一部が他の方法で仕向地へ継搬される場合には、積荷利害関係人に通知することが実際的であれば通知することを条件として、共同海損における権利および責任は、運送契約および適用される法律の下で正当化できる範囲において、あたかも航海は当初の船舶で継続したものとして、かかる継搬はなかったものと仮定したときの権利および責任にできる限り近いものとする。 | |
| 本条第3項を適用することにより、共同海損に認容される金額のうち積荷に割り当てる金額は、荷主が積荷を自己の費用で継搬したとすれば要する費用を超えてはならない。 | |

## York-Antwerp Rules 1994

Rule I. Jettison of Cargo
No jettison of cargo shall be made good as general average, unless such cargo is carried in accordance with the recognised custom of the trade.

Rule II. **Loss or Damage by Sacrifices** for the Common Safety
**Loss of or damage to the property involved in the common maritime adventure** by or in consequence of a sacrifice made for the common safety, and by water which goes down a ship's hatches opened or other opening made for the purpose of making a jettison for the common safety, shall be made good as general average.

Rule III. Extinguishing Fire on Shipboard
Damage done to a ship and cargo, or either of them, by water or otherwise, including damage by beaching or scuttling a burning ship, in extinguishing a fire on board the ship, shall be made good as general average; except that no compensation shall be made for damage by smoke however caused **or by heat of the fire.**

## York-Antwerp Rules 1974 as amended 1990

Rule I. Jettison of Cargo
No jettison of cargo shall be made good as general average, unless such cargo is carried in accordance with the recognised custom of the trade.

Rule II. Damage by Jettison and Sacrifice for the Common Safety
Damage done to a ship and cargo, or either of them, by or in consequence of a sacrifice made for the common safety, and by water which goes down a ship's hatches opened or other opening made for the purpose of making a jettison for the common safety, shall be made good as general average.

Rule III. Extinguishing Fire on Shipboard
Damage done to a ship and cargo, or either of them, by water or otherwise, including damage by beaching or scuttling a burning ship, in extinguishing a fire on board the ship, shall be made good as general average; except that no compensation shall be made for damage by smoke or heat however caused.

| 1994年ヨーク・アントワープ規則 | 1990年修正<br>1974年ヨーク・アントワープ規則 |
|---|---|
| **I条 投荷**<br>　投荷は、その積荷が承認された商慣習に従い運送されたものでなければ、共同海損としててん補しない。 | **I条 投荷**<br>　投荷は、その積荷が承認された商慣習に従い運送されたものでなければ、共同海損としててん補しない。 |
| **II条　共同の安全のための犠牲による滅失または損傷**<br>　共同の安全のために行った犠牲により、もしくは犠牲の結果として、または共同の安全のために投荷を行う目的で開いたハッチもしくはその目的で作った他の開口部から浸入した水により、共同の航海団体を構成する財産に生じた滅失または損傷は、これを共同海損としててん補する。 | **II条　共同の安全のための投荷または犠牲による損害**<br>　共同の安全のために行った犠牲により、もしくは犠牲の結果として、または共同の安全のために投荷を行う目的で開いたハッチもしくはその目的で作った他の開口部から浸入した水により、船舶および積荷またはそのいずれかに生じた損害は、これを共同海損としててん補する。 |
| **III条　船火事の消火**<br>　船火事の消火にあたって、注水またはその他の方法により、船舶および積荷またはそのいずれかに生じた損害は、火災中の船舶を浅瀬に乗り揚げさせるか、または穿孔することによる損害とともに、これを共同海損としててん補する。ただし、原因のいかんを問わず煙により生じた損害または火災の熱により生じた損害はてん補しない。 | **III条　船火事の消火**<br>　船火事の消火にあたって、注水またはその他の方法により、船舶および積荷またはそのいずれかに生じた損害は、火災中の船舶を浅瀬に乗り揚げさせるか、または穿孔することによる損害とともに、これを共同海損としててん補する。ただし、原因のいかんを問わず煙または熱により生じた損害はてん補しない。 |

## York-Antwerp Rules 1994

### Rule IV. Cutting Away Wreck

Loss or damage sustained by cutting away wreck or parts of the ship which have been previously carried away or are effectively lost by accident shall not be made good as general average.

### Rule V. Voluntary Stranding

When a ship is intentionally run on shore for the common safety, whether or not she might have been driven on shore, the consequent loss or damage **to the property involved in the common maritime adventure** shall be allowed in general average.

### Rule VI. Salvage Remuneration

(a) Expenditure incurred by the parties to the adventure in the nature of salvage, whether under contract or otherwise, shall be allowed in general average provided that the salvage operations were carried out for the purpose of preserving from peril the property involved in the common maritime adventure.

## York-Antwerp Rules 1974 as amended 1990

### Rule IV. Cutting Away Wreck

Loss or damage sustained by cutting away wreck or parts of the ship which have been previously carried away or are effectively lost by accident shall not be made good as general average.

### Rule V. Voluntary Stranding

When a ship is intentionally run on shore for the common safety, whether or not she might have been driven on shore, the consequent loss or damage shall be allowed in general average.

### Rule VI. Salvage Remuneration

(a) Expenditure incurred by the parties to the adventure in the nature of salvage, whether under contract or otherwise, shall be allowed in general average provided that the salvage operations were carried out for the purpose of preserving from peril the property involved in the common maritime adventure.

| 1994年ヨーク・アントワープ規則 | 1990年修正<br>1974年ヨーク・アントワープ規則 |
|---|---|
| Ⅳ条　難破物の切除<br>　事故によりすでに切り離されるか、または実質上滅失した状態にある難破物または船体の一部を切除することにより生じた滅失または損傷は、共同海損としててん補しない。 | Ⅳ条　難破物の切除<br>　事故によりすでに切り離されるか、または実質上滅失した状態にある難破物または船体の一部を切除することにより生じた滅失または損傷は、共同海損としててん補しない。 |
| Ⅴ条　任意の乗り揚げ<br>　共同の安全のために船舶が故意に乗り揚げた場合は、乗り揚げが不可避であったか否かを問わず、これにより共同の航海団体を構成する財産に生じた滅失または損傷は、共同海損に認容する。 | Ⅴ条　任意の乗り揚げ<br>　共同の安全のために船舶が故意に乗り揚げた場合は、乗り揚げが不可避であったか否かを問わず、これにより生じた滅失または損傷は、共同海損に認容する。 |
| Ⅵ条　救助報酬<br>　(a)　航海団体関係人が負担する救助の性質を有する費用は、契約に基づくと否とを問わず、救助行為が共同の航海団体を構成する財産を危険から守る意図でなされた場合には、これを共同海損に認容する。 | Ⅵ条　救助報酬<br>　(a)　航海団体関係人が負担する救助の性質を有する費用は、契約に基づくと否とを問わず、救助行為が共同の航海団体を構成する財産を危険から守る意図でなされた場合には、これを共同海損に認容する。 |

## York-Antwerp Rules 1994

Expenditure allowed in general average shall include any salvage remuneration in which the skill and efforts of the salvors in preventing or minimising damage to the environment such as is referred to in Art.13 paragraph 1(b) of the International Convention on Salvage, 1989 have been taken into account.

(b) Special compensation payable to a salvor by the shipowner under Art.14 of the said Convention to the extent specified in paragraph 4 of that Article or under any other provision similar in substance shall not be allowed in general average.

Rule VII. Damage to Machinery and Boilers
Damage caused to any machinery and boilers of a ship which is ashore and in a position of peril, in endeavouring to refloat, shall be allowed in general average when shown to have arisen from an actual intention to float the ship for the common safety at the risk of such damage; but where a ship is afloat no loss or damage caused by working the propelling machinery and boilers shall in any circumstances be made good as general average.

## York-Antwerp Rules 1974 as amended 1990

Expenditure allowed in general average shall include any salvage remuneration in which the skill and efforts of the salvors in preventing or minimising damage to the environment such as is referred to in Art.13 paragraph 1(b) of the International Convention on Salvage, 1989 have been taken into account.

(b) Special compensation payable to a salvor by the shipowner under Art.14 of the said Convention to the extent specified in paragraph 4 of that Article or under any other provision similar in substance shall not be allowed in general average.

Rule VII. Damage to Machinery and Boilers
Damage caused to any machinery and boilers of a ship which is ashore and in a position of peril, in endeavouring to refloat, shall be allowed in general average when shown to have arisen from an actual intention to float the ship for the common safety at the risk of such damage; but where a ship is afloat no loss or damage caused by working the propelling machinery and boilers shall in any circumstances be made good as general average.

| 1994年ヨーク・アントワープ規則 | 1990年修正<br>1974年ヨーク・アントワープ規則 |
|---|---|
| 　共同海損に認容される費用には、1989年海難救助に関する国際条約第13条第1項(b)に規定されているような環境損害を防止または軽減するための救助者の技能および努力が勘案された一切の救助報酬を含むものとする。 | 　共同海損に認容される費用には、1989年海難救助に関する国際条約第13条第1項(b)に規定されているような環境損害を防止または軽減するための救助者の技能および努力が勘案された一切の救助報酬を含むものとする。 |
| 　(b)　同条約第14条第4項に規定されている範囲内で同条約第14条に基づいて、またはその他の実質的に同様の規定に基づいて、船主が救助者に支払うべき特別補償は、共同海損に認容しない。 | 　(b)　同条約第14条第4項に規定されている範囲内で同条約第14条に基づいて、またはその他の実質的に同様の規定に基づいて、船主が救助者に支払うべき特別補償は、共同海損に認容しない。 |
| VII条　機械およびボイラーの損害<br>　乗り揚げて危険な状態にある船舶を浮揚させようと努めるにあたり生じた機械およびボイラーの損害は、いかなる機械またはボイラーについてのものであれ、その損害を覚悟したうえで、共同の安全のために船舶を浮揚させようとする現実の意図から生じたものであることが証明された場合には、これを共同海損に認容する。ただし、船舶が浮揚している場合には、推進機関およびボイラーを使用することにより生じた滅失または損傷は、いかなる場合にも共同海損としててん補しない。 | VII条　機械およびボイラーの損害<br>　乗り揚げて危険な状態にある船舶を浮揚させようと努めるにあたり生じた機械およびボイラーの損害は、いかなる機械またはボイラーについてのものであれ、その損害を覚悟したうえで、共同の安全のために船舶を浮揚させようとする現実の意図から生じたものであることが証明された場合には、これを共同海損に認容する。ただし、船舶が浮揚している場合には、推進機関およびボイラーを使用することにより生じた滅失または損傷は、いかなる場合にも共同海損としててん補しない。 |

## York-Antwerp Rules 1994

Rule VIII. Expenses lightening a Ship when Ashore, and Consequent Damage

When a ship is ashore and cargo and ship's fuel and stores or any of them are discharged as a general average act, the extra cost of lightening, lighter hire and reshipping (if incurred), and **any loss or damage to the property involved in the common maritime adventure in consequence thereof,** shall be admitted as general average.

Rule IX. **Cargo,** Ship's Materials and Stores Used for Fuel

**Cargo,** ship's materials and stores, or any of them, necessarily **used** for fuel for the common safety at a time of peril shall be admitted as general average, **but when such an allowance is made for the cost of ship's materials and stores the general average shall be credited with the estimated cost of the fuel which would otherwise have been consumed in prosecuting the intended voyage.**

## York-Antwerp Rules 1974 as amended 1990

Rule VIII. Expenses lightening a Ship when Ashore, and Consequent Damage

When a ship is ashore and cargo and ship's fuel and stores or any of them are discharged as a general average act, the extra cost of lightening, lighter hire and reshipping (if incurred), and the loss or damage sustained thereby, shall be admitted as general average.

Rule IX. Ship's Materials and Stores Burnt for Fuel

Ship's materials and stores, or any of them, necessarily burnt for fuel for the common safety at a time of peril, shall be admitted as general average, when and only when an ample supply of fuel had been provided; but the estimated quantity of fuel that would have been consumed, calculated at the price current at the ship's last port of departure at the date of her leaving, shall be credited to the general average.

## 1994年ヨーク・アントワープ規則

VIII条　乗り揚げた船舶の船脚を軽くする費用およびその結果生じた損害

　船舶が乗り揚げて、積荷、船舶の燃料および貯蔵品またはそのいずれかを共同海損行為として荷揚げした場合には、余分に要した船脚軽減、艀の使用および（再積込みしたときは）再積込みのための費用、ならびにこの結果として共同の航海団体を構成する財産に生じた滅失または損傷は、共同海損として認容する。

IX条　燃料として使用した積荷、船用品および貯蔵品

　危険な時にあたり共同の安全のために、やむをえず燃料として使用した積荷、船用品および貯蔵品またはそのいずれかは、共同海損として認容する。ただし、船用品および貯蔵品の費用が認容されるときは、もしそれを使用しなければ、予定の航海において消費されたであろう燃料の費用の見積額は、共同海損から控除する。

## 1990年修正 1974年ヨーク・アントワープ規則

VIII条　乗り揚げた船舶の船脚を軽くする費用およびその結果生じた損害

　船舶が乗り揚げて、積荷、船舶の燃料および貯蔵品またはそのいずれかを共同海損行為として荷揚げした場合には、余分に要した船脚軽減、艀の使用および（再積込みしたときは）再積込みのための費用、ならびにこれによって被った滅失または損傷は、共同海損として認容する。

IX条　燃料としてたいた船用品および貯蔵品

　危険な時にあたり共同の安全のために、やむをえず燃料としてたいた船用品および貯蔵品またはそのいずれかは、船舶が十分な燃料を用意していた場合に限り、共同海損として認容する。ただし、消費されたであろう燃料の見積量は、船舶の最後の発航港における発航日の時価で計算し、共同海損から控除する。

## York-Antwerp Rules 1994

Rule X. Expenses at Port of Refuge, etc.

(a) When a ship shall have entered a port or place of refuge or shall have returned to her port or place of loading in consequence of accident, sacrifice or other extraordinary circumstances which render that necessary for the common safety, the expenses of entering such port or place shall be admitted as general average; and when she shall have sailed thence with her original cargo, or a part of it, the corresponding expenses of leaving such port or place consequent upon such entry or return shall likewise be admitted as general average.

When a ship is at any port or place of refuge and is necessarily removed to another port or place because repairs cannot be carried out in the first port or place, the provisions of this Rule shall be applied to the second port or place as if it were a port or place of refuge and the cost of such removal including temporary repairs and towage shall be admitted as general average. The provisions of Rule XI shall be applied to the prolongation of the voyage occasioned by such removal.

## York-Antwerp Rules 1974 as amended 1990

Rule X. Expenses at Port of Refuge, etc.

(a) When a ship shall have entered a port or place of refuge, or shall have returned to her port or place of loading in consequence of accident, sacrifice or other extraordinary circumstances, which render that necessary for the common safety, the expenses of entering such port or place shall be admitted as general average; and when she shall have sailed thence with her original cargo, or a part of it, the corresponding expenses of leaving such port or place consequent upon such entry or return shall likewise be admitted as general average.

When a ship is at any port or place of refuge and is necessarily removed to another port or place because repairs cannot be carried out in the first port or place, the provisions of this Rule shall be applied to the second port or place as if it were a port or place of refuge and the cost of such removal including temporary repairs and towage shall be admitted as general average. The provisions of Rule XI shall be applied to the prolongation of the voyage occasioned by such removal.

## 1994年ヨーク・アントワープ規則

X条　避難港その他における費用

　(a)　事故、犠牲またはその他の異常な事情の結果、船舶が共同の安全のためにやむなく避難港もしくは避難地に入り、または船積港もしくは船積地に帰るときは、その港または地に入航する費用は、共同海損として認容する。さらに、その船舶がもとの積荷またはその一部を積載して出るときは、入港または帰港の結果生じた出航する費用も同様に、共同海損として認容する。

　船舶が避難港または避難地にいて、そこで修繕ができないために、やむをえず他の港または他の地に回航する場合には、前項の規定は第2の港または第2の地についても、避難港または避難地におけると同様に適用し、その回航に要する費用は、仮修繕費および曳航費を含め、共同海損として認容する。XI条の規定はこのような回航により生じる航海の延長に適用する。

## 1990年修正
## 1974年ヨーク・アントワープ規則

X条　避難港その他における費用

　(a)　事故、犠牲またはその他の異常な事情の結果、船舶が共同の安全のためにやむなく避難港もしくは避難地に入り、または船積港もしくは船積地に帰るときは、その港または地に入航する費用は、共同海損として認容する。さらに、その船舶がもとの積荷またはその一部を積載して出るときは、入港または帰港の結果生じた出航する費用も同様に、共同海損として認容する。

　船舶が避難港または避難地にいて、そこで修繕ができないために、やむをえず他の港または他の地に回航する場合には、前項の規定は第2の港または第2の地についても、避難港または避難地におけると同様に適用し、その回航に要する費用は、仮修繕費および曳航費を含め、共同海損として認容する。XI条の規定はこのような回航により生じる航海の延長に適用する。

## York-Antwerp Rules 1994

(b) The cost of handling on board or discharging cargo, fuel or stores whether at a port or place of loading, call or refuge, shall be admitted as general average, when the handling or discharge was necessary for the common safety or to enable damage to the ship caused by sacrifice or accident to be repaired, if the repairs were necessary for the safe prosecution of the voyage, except in cases where the damage to the ship is discovered at a port or place of loading or call without any accident or other extraordinary circumstances connected with such damage having taken place during the voyage.

The cost of handling on board or discharging cargo, fuel or stores shall not be admissible as general average when incurred solely for the purpose of restowage due to shifting during the voyage, unless such restowage is necessary for the common safety.

## York-Antwerp Rules 1974 as amended 1990

(b) The cost of handling on board or discharging cargo, fuel or stores whether at a port or place of loading, call or refuge, shall be admitted as general average, when the handling or discharge was necessary for the common safety or to enable damage to the ship caused by sacrifice or accident to be repaired, if the repairs were necessary for the safe prosecution of the voyage, except in cases where the damage to the ship is discovered at a port or place of loading or call without any accident or other extraordinary circumstances connected with such damage having taken place during the voyage.

The cost of handling on board or discharging cargo, fuel or stores shall not be admissible as general average when incurred solely for the purpose of restowage due to shifting during the voyage, unless such restowage is necessary for the common safety.

### 1994年ヨーク・アントワープ規則

　(b)　船積み、寄航または避難の港もしくは地のいずれにあるかを問わず、積荷、燃料または貯蔵品の荷繰りまたは荷揚げの費用は、その荷繰りまたは荷揚げが共同の安全のために必要であるか、または犠牲もしくは事故により生じた船舶の損傷の修繕が航海の安全な遂行のために必要な場合に、その修繕を可能にするためにその荷繰りまたは荷揚げが必要なときは、これを共同海損として認容する。ただし、船舶の損傷が船積みまたは寄航の港もしくは地で発見され、その損傷と関連のある事故またはその他の異常な事情が航海中に発生していない場合は、この限りでない。

　積荷、燃料または貯蔵品の荷繰りまたは荷揚げの費用が、単に航海中の荷崩れに起因する再積付けのために支出された場合は、その再積付けが共同の安全のために必要でない限り、共同海損として認容しない。

### 1990年修正
### 1974年ヨーク・アントワープ規則

　(b)　船積み、寄航または避難の港もしくは地のいずれにあるかを問わず、積荷、燃料または貯蔵品の荷繰りまたは荷揚げの費用は、その荷繰りまたは荷揚げが共同の安全のために必要であるか、または犠牲もしくは事故により生じた船舶の損傷の修繕が航海の安全な遂行のために必要な場合に、その修繕を可能にするためにその荷繰りまたは荷揚げが必要なときは、これを共同海損として認容する。ただし、船舶の損傷が船積みまたは寄航の港もしくは地で発見され、その損傷と関連のある事故またはその他の異常な事情が航海中に発生していない場合は、この限りでない。

　積荷、燃料または貯蔵品の荷繰りまたは荷揚げの費用が、単に航海中の荷崩れに起因する再積付けのために支出された場合は、その再積付けが共同の安全のために必要でない限り、共同海損として認容しない。

## York-Antwerp Rules 1994

(c) Whenever the cost of handling or discharging cargo, fuel or stores is admissible as general average, the costs of storage, including insurance if reasonably incurred, reloading and stowing of such cargo, fuel or stores shall likewise be admitted as general average. **The provisions of Rule XI shall be applied to the extra period of detention occasioned by such reloading or restowing.**

But when the ship is condemned or does not proceed on her original voyage, storage expenses shall be admitted as general average only up to the date of the ship's condemnation or of the abandonment of the voyage or up to the date of completion of discharge of cargo if the condemnation or abandonment takes place before that date.

## York-Antwerp Rules 1974 as amended 1990

(c) Whenever the cost of handling or discharging cargo, fuel or stores is admissible as general average, the costs of storage, including insurance if reasonably incurred, reloading and stowing of such cargo, fuel or stores shall likewise be admitted as general average.

But when the ship is condemned or does not proceed on her original voyage, storage expenses shall be admitted as general average only up to the date of the ship's condemnation or of the abandonment of the voyage or up to the date of completion of discharge of cargo if the condemnation or abandonment takes place before that date.

## 1994 年ヨーク・アントワープ規則

　(c)　積荷、燃料または貯蔵品の荷繰りまたは荷揚げの費用が共同海損として認容される場合は、その積荷、燃料または貯蔵品の合理的に支出された保険料を含む保管料、再積込みおよび再積付けの費用も同様に、これを共同海損として認容する。XI 条の規定は、このような再積込みまたは再積付けによって生じた余分の滞泊期間に適用する。

　ただし、船舶が不適航の宣告を受けるか、または当初の航海を継続しない場合は、保管の費用は、船舶の不適航の宣告もしくは航海の放棄の日、またはもし不適航の宣告もしくは航海の放棄が積荷の荷揚げ完了前に行われた場合には、積荷の荷揚げ完了日まで、これを共同海損として認容する。

## 1990 年修正 1974 年ヨーク・アントワープ規則

　(c)　積荷、燃料または貯蔵品の荷繰りまたは荷揚げの費用が共同海損として認容される場合は、その積荷、燃料または貯蔵品の合理的に支出された保険料を含む保管料、再積込みおよび再積付けの費用も同様に、これを共同海損として認容する。

　ただし、船舶が不適航の宣告を受けるか、または当初の航海を継続しない場合は、保管の費用は、船舶の不適航の宣告もしくは航海の放棄の日、またはもし不適航の宣告もしくは航海の放棄が積荷の荷揚げ完了前に行われた場合には、積荷の荷揚げ完了日まで、これを共同海損として認容する。

## York-Antwerp Rules 1994

Rule XI. Wages and Maintenance of Crew and Other Expenses Bearing up for and in a Port of Refuge, etc.

(a) Wages and maintenance of master, officers and crew reasonably incurred and fuel and stores consumed during the prolongation of the voyage occasioned by a ship entering a port or place of refuge or returning to her port or place of loading shall be admitted as general average when the expenses of entering such port or place are allowable in general average in accordance with Rule X (a).

(b) When a ship shall have entered or been detained in any port or place in consequence of accident, sacrifice or other extraordinary circumstances which render that necessary for the common safety, or to enable damage to the ship caused by sacrifice or accident to be repaired, if the repairs were necessary for the safe prosecution of the voyage, the wages and maintenance of the master, officers and crew reasonably incurred during the extra period of detention in such port or place until the ship shall or should have been made ready to proceed upon her voyage, shall be admitted in general average.

## York-Antwerp Rules 1974 as amended 1990

Rule XI. Wages and Maintenance of Crew and other Expenses bearing up for and in a Port of Refuge, etc.

(a) Wages and maintenance of master, officers and crew reasonably incurred and fuel and stores consumed during the prolongation of the voyage occasioned by a ship entering a port or place of refuge or returning to her port or place of loading shall be admitted as general average when the expenses of entering such port or place are allowable in general average in accordance with Rule X (a).

(b) When a ship shall have entered or been detained in any port or place in consequence of accident, sacrifice or other extraordinary circumstances which render that necessary for the common safety, or to enable damage to the ship caused by sacrifice or accident to be repaired, if the repairs were necessary for the safe prosecution of the voyage, the wages and maintenance of the master, officers and crew reasonably incurred during the extra period of detention in such port or place until the ship shall or should have been made ready to proceed upon her voyage, shall be admitted in general average.

| 1994年ヨーク・アントワープ規則 | 1990年修正<br>1974年ヨーク・アントワープ規則 |
|---|---|
| XI条　避難港その他への転針の間および避難港その他にある間の船員の給料および扶養料ならびにその他の費用<br><br>　(a)　船舶が避難港もしくは避難地に入り、または船積港もしくは船積地に帰ることにより生ずる航海の延長の間に正当に支払った船長、職員および部員の給料および扶養料、ならびに消費された燃料および貯蔵品は、その港または地に入る費用がX条(a)に従い共同海損に認容される場合には、これを共同海損として認容する。<br><br>　(b)　事故、犠牲もしくはその他の異常な事情の結果、共同の安全のためやむなく、または犠牲もしくは事故により生じた船舶の損傷の修繕が航海の安全な遂行のため必要なとき、その修繕を可能にするために船舶がいずれかの港またはいずれかの地に入りまたは滞泊したときは、その港または地において余分の滞泊期間中に正当に支払った船長、職員および部員の給料および扶養料は、船舶が当初の航海を継続する準備ができた時、またはできたであろう時まで、これを共同海損に認容する。 | XI条　避難港その他への転針の間および避難港その他にある間の船員の給料および扶養料ならびにその他の費用<br><br>　(a)　船舶が避難港もしくは避難地に入り、または船積港もしくは船積地に帰ることにより生ずる航海の延長の間に正当に支払った船長、職員および部員の給料および扶養料、ならびに消費された燃料および貯蔵品は、その港または地に入る費用がX条(a)に従い共同海損に認容される場合には、これを共同海損として認容する。<br><br>　(b)　事故、犠牲もしくはその他の異常な事情の結果、共同の安全のためやむなく、または犠牲もしくは事故により生じた船舶の損傷の修繕が航海の安全な遂行のため必要なとき、その修繕を可能にするために船舶がいずれかの港またはいずれかの地に入りまたは滞泊したときは、その港または地において余分の滞泊期間中に正当に支払った船長、職員および部員の給料および扶養料は、船舶が当初の航海を継続する準備ができた時、またはできたであろう時まで、これを共同海損に認容する。 |

## York-Antwerp Rules 1994

Fuel and stores consumed during the extra period of detention shall be admitted as general average, except such fuel and stores as are consumed in effecting repairs not allowable in general average.

Port charges incurred during the extra period of detention shall likewise be admitted as general average except such charges as are incurred solely by reason of repairs not allowable in general average.

## York-Antwerp Rules 1974 as amended 1990

Provided that when damage to the ship is discovered at a port or place of loading or call without any accident or other extraordinary circumstance connected with such damage having taken place during the voyage, then the wages and maintenance of master, officers and crew and fuel and stores consumed during the extra detention for repairs to damages so discovered shall not be admissible as general average, even if the repairs are necessary for the safe prosecution of the voyage.

When the ship is condemned or does not proceed on her original voyage, wages and maintenance of the master, officers and crew and fuel and stores consumed shall be admitted as general average only up to the date of the ship's condemnation or of the abandonment of the voyage or up to the date of completion of discharge of cargo if the condemnation or abandonment takes place before that date.

XI 条 (b)

| 1994 年ヨーク・アントワープ規則 | 1990 年修正<br>1974 年ヨーク・アントワープ規則 |
|---|---|
| 　余分の滞泊期間中に消費した燃料および貯蔵品は、共同海損として認容する。ただし、共同海損に認容されない修繕を施工するために消費した燃料および貯蔵品は除く。 | 　ただし、船舶の損傷が船積みまたは寄航の港もしくは地で発見された場合に、その損傷と関連のある事故またはその他の異常な事情が航海中に発生していないときは、このようにして発見された損傷の修繕のために要した余分の滞泊期間中の船長、職員および部員の給料および扶養料、ならびに消費された燃料および貯蔵品は、修繕が航海の安全な遂行のために必要な場合といえども、共同海損として認容しない。 |
| 　余分の滞泊期間中に支出した港費も同様に、共同海損として認容する。ただし、共同海損に認容されない修繕のためにのみ支出した港費は除く。 | 　船舶が不適航の宣告を受けるか、または当初の航海を継続しない場合は、船長、職員および部員の給料および扶養料、ならびに消費された燃料および貯蔵品は、船舶の不適航の宣告もしくは航海の放棄の日まで、またはもし不適航の宣告もしくは航海の放棄が積荷の荷揚げ完了前に行われた場合には積荷の荷揚げ完了日まで、これを共同海損として認容する。 |

## York-Antwerp Rules 1994

Provided that when damage to the ship is discovered at a port or place of loading or call without any accident or other extraordinary circumstance connected with such damage having taken place during the voyage, then the wages and maintenance of master, officers and crew and fuel and stores consumed **and port charges incurred** during the extra detention for repairs to damages so discovered shall not be admissible as general average, even if the repairs are necessary for the safe prosecution of the voyage.

When the ship is condemned or does not proceed on her original voyage, **the** wages and maintenance of the master, officers and crew and fuel and stores consumed **and port charges** shall be admitted as general average only up to the date of the ship's condemnation or of the abandonment of the voyage or up to the date of completion of discharge of cargo if the condemnation or abandonment takes place before that date.

(c) For the purpose of this and the other Rules wages shall include all payments made to or for the benefit of the master, officers and crew, whether such payments be imposed by law upon the shipowners or be made under the terms **of** articles of employment.

## York-Antwerp Rules 1974 as amended 1990

Fuel and stores consumed during the extra period of detention shall be admitted as general average, except such fuel and stores as are consumed in effecting repairs not allowable in general average.

Port charges incurred during the extra period of detention shall likewise be admitted as general average except such charges as are incurred solely by reason of repairs not allowable in general average.

(c) For the purpose of this and the other Rules wages shall include all payments made to or for the benefit of the master, officers and crew, whether such payments be imposed by law upon the shipowners or be made under the terms or articles of employment.

| 1994年ヨーク・アントワープ規則 | 1990年修正<br>1974年ヨーク・アントワープ規則 |

ただし、船舶の損傷か船積みまたは寄航の港もしくは地で発見された場合に、その損傷と関連のある事故またはその他の異常な事情が航海中に発生していないときは、このようにして発見された損傷の修繕のために要した余分の滞泊期間中の船長、職員および部員の給料および扶養料、消費された燃料および貯蔵品ならびに支出された港費は、修繕が航海の安全な遂行のために必要な場合といえども、共同海損として認容しない。

余分の滞泊期間中に消費した燃料および貯蔵品は、共同海損として認容する。ただし、共同海損に認容されない修繕を施工するために消費した燃料および貯蔵品は除く。

船舶が不適航の宣告を受けるか、または当初の航海を継続しない場合は、船長、職員および部員の給料および扶養料、消費された燃料および貯蔵品ならびに港費は、船舶の不適航の宣告もしくは航海の放棄の日まで、またはもし不適航の宣告もしくは航海の放棄が積荷の荷揚げ完了前に行われた場合には積荷の荷揚げ完了日まで、これを共同海損として認容する。

余分の滞泊期間中に支出した港費も同様に、共同海損として認容する。ただし、共同海損に認容されない修繕のためにのみ支出した港費は除く。

(c) 本条および他の規定において給料とは、船長、職員および部員に対し、またはそれらのためになしたすべての支払いを含むものとし、その支払いが法律により船主に課されたか、または雇傭契約の条項の下になされたかを問わないものとする。

(c) 本条および他の規定において給料とは、船長、職員および部員に対し、またはそれらのためになしたすべての支払いを含むものとし、その支払いが法律により船主に課されたか、または雇傭の条件もしくは条項の下になされたかを問わないものとする。

## York-Antwerp Rules 1994

(d) **The cost of measures undertaken to prevent or minimise damage to the environment shall be allowed in general average when incurred in any or all of the following circumstances:**

(i) **as part of an operation performed for the common safety which, had it been undertaken by a party outside the common maritime adventure, would have entitled such party to a salvage reward;**

(ii) **as a condition of entry into or departure from any port or place in the circumstances prescribed in Rule X(a);**

(iii) **as a condition of remaining at any port or place in the circumstances prescribed in Rule XI(b), provided that when there is an actual escape or release of pollutant substances the cost of any additional measures required on that account to prevent or minimise pollution or environmental damage shall not be allowed as general average;**

(iv) **necessarily in connection with the discharging, storing or reloading of cargo whenever the cost of those operations is admissible as general average.**

## York-Antwerp Rules 1974 as amended 1990

(d) When overtime is paid to the master, officers or crew for maintenance of the ship or repairs, the cost of which is not allowable in general average, such overtime shall be allowed in general average only up to the saving in expense which would have been incurred and admitted as general average, had such overtime not been incurred.

## XI 条 (d)

| 1994 年ヨーク・アントワープ規則 | 1990 年修正<br>1974 年ヨーク・アントワープ規則 |
|---|---|
| (d) 環境損害を防止または軽減するためにとられた措置に要した費用は、次のいずれか、またはすべての状況の下で支出された場合には、共同海損に認容する。<br><br>(i) 共同の安全のためになされた作業の一部であって、もし共同の航海団体関係人以外の者が行ったとすれば、その者が救助報酬を請求することができるような作業である場合。<br><br>(ii) X 条 (a) に定められた状況において、ある港またはある地に入るための、またはそこから出るための条件である場合。<br><br>(iii) XI 条 (b) に定められた状況において、ある港またはある地に滞泊するための条件である場合。ただし、汚染物質の現実の流出または排出があるときには、そのことによって汚染または環境損害を防止または軽減するために必要ないかなる追加的措置がとられても、その費用は共同海損として認容しない。<br><br>(iv) 積荷の荷揚げ、倉入れまたは再積込み作業が共同海損として認容されるときに、これらの作業に関連してやむをえず支出されたものである場合。 | (d) それに要する費用が共同海損に認容されない船舶の保守または修繕のために、船長、職員および部員に対し超過勤務手当を支払ったときは、その超過勤務手当は、もしそれが支出されなかったならば代わりに支出され、かつ共同海損として認容されたであろう費用が節約された限度において、これを共同海損に認容する。 |

## York- Antwerp Rules 1994

Rule XII. Damage to Cargo in Discharging, etc.

Damage to or loss of cargo, fuel or stores **sustained in consequence of their** handling, discharging, storing, reloading and stowing shall be made good as general average, when and only when the cost of those measures respectively is admitted as general average.

Rule XIII. Deductions from Cost of Repairs

Repairs to be allowed in general average shall not be subject to deductions in respect of "new for old" where old material or parts are replaced by new unless the ship is over fifteen years old in which case there shall be a deduction of one third. The deductions shall be regulated by the age of the ship from the 31st December of the year of completion of construction to the date of the general average act, except for insulation, life and similar boats, communications and navigational apparatus and equipment, machinery and boilers for which the deductions shall be regulated by the age of the particular parts to which they apply.

The deductions shall be made only from the cost of the new material or parts when finished and ready to be installed in the ship.

## York-Antwerp Rules 1974 as amended 1990

Rule XII. Damage to Cargo in Discharging, etc.

Damage to or loss of cargo, fuel or stores caused in the act of handling, discharging, storing, reloading and stowing shall be made good as general average, when and only when the cost of those measures respectively is admitted as general average.

Rule XIII. Deductions from Cost of Repairs

Repairs to be allowed in general average shall not be subject to deductions in respect of "new for old" where old material or parts are replaced by new unless the ship is over fifteen years old in which case there shall be a deduction of one third. The deductions shall be regulated by the age of the ship from the 31st December of the year of completion of construction to the date of the general average act, except for insulation, life and similar boats, communications and navigational apparatus and equipment, machinery and boilers for which the deductions shall be regulated by the age of the particular parts to which they apply.

The deductions shall be made only from the cost of the new material or parts when finished and ready to be installed in the ship.

| 1994年ヨーク・アントワープ規則 | 1990年修正<br>1974年ヨーク・アントワープ規則 |
|---|---|
| XII条　荷揚げその他にあたり積荷に生じた損害<br>　荷繰り、荷揚げ、倉入れ、再積込みおよび積付けの結果被った積荷、燃料または貯蔵品の損傷または滅失は、その措置に要する費用がそれぞれ共同海損として認容される場合に限り、これを共同海損としててん補する。 | XII条　荷揚げその他にあたり積荷に生じた損害<br>　荷繰り、荷揚げ、倉入れ、再積込みおよび積付けを行うにあたり生じた積荷、燃料または貯蔵品の損傷または滅失は、その措置に要する費用がそれぞれ共同海損として認容される場合に限り、これを共同海損としててん補する。 |
| XIII条　修繕費からの控除<br>　共同海損に認容すべき修繕費については、旧材料または旧部品が新替された場合の「新旧交換」に関する控除を行わない。ただし、船齢が15年を超える場合には、3分の1の控除を行う。控除は建造完了の年の12月31日から共同海損行為の日までの船齢により定める。ただし、防熱材、救命艇および類似の端艇、通信および航海計器または装置、機械ならびにボイラーについては、控除の適用される特定の部品の年数により控除を行う。<br><br>　控除は、仕上げを完了し船舶に取付ける準備ができた時点における新材料代または新部品代についてのみ行う。 | XIII条　修繕費からの控除<br>　共同海損に認容すべき修繕費については、旧材料または旧部品が新替された場合の「新旧交換」に関する控除を行わない。ただし、船齢が15年を超える場合には、3分の1の控除を行う。控除は建造完了の年の12月31日から共同海損行為の日までの船齢により定める。ただし、防熱材、救命艇および類似の端艇、通信および航海計器または装置、機械ならびにボイラーについては、控除の適用される特定の部品の年数により控除を行う。<br><br>　控除は、仕上げを完了し船舶に取付ける準備ができた時点における新材料代または新部品代についてのみ行う。 |

## York- Antwerp Rules 1994

No deduction shall be made in respect of provisions, stores, anchors and chain cables.

Drydock and slipway dues and costs of shifting the ship shall be allowed in full.

The costs of cleaning, painting or coating of bottom shall not be allowed in general average unless the bottom has been painted or coated within the twelve months preceding the date of the general average act in which case one half of such costs shall be allowed.

Rule XIV. Temporary Repairs
Where temporary repairs are effected to a ship at a port of loading, call or refuge, for the common safety, or of damage caused by general average sacrifice, the cost of such repairs shall be admitted as general average.

Where temporary repairs of accidental damage are effected in order to enable the adventure to be completed, the cost of such repairs shall be admitted as general average without regard to the saving, if any, to other interests, but only up to the saving in expense which would have been incurred and allowed in general average if such repairs had not been effected there.

## York-Antwerp Rules 1974 as amended 1990

No deduction shall be made in respect of provisions, stores, anchors and chain cables.

Drydock and slipway dues and costs of shifting the ship shall be allowed in full.

The costs of cleaning, painting or coating of bottom shall not be allowed in general average unless the bottom has been painted or coated within the twelve months preceding the date of the general average act in which case one half of such costs shall be allowed.

Rule XIV. Temporary Repairs
Where temporary repairs are effected to a ship at a port of loading, call or refuge, for the common safety, or of damage caused by general average sacrifice, the cost of such repairs shall be admitted as general average.

Where temporary repairs of accidental damage are effected in order to enable the adventure to be completed, the cost of such repairs shall be admitted as general average without regard to the saving, if any, to other interests, but only up to the saving in expense which would have been incurred and allowed in general average if such repairs had not been effected there.

| 1994年ヨーク・アントワープ規則 | 1990年修正<br>1974年ヨーク・アントワープ規則 |
|---|---|
| 　食料品、貯蔵品、錨および錨鎖については、控除を行わない。 | 　食料品、貯蔵品、錨および錨鎖については、控除を行わない。 |
| 　入出渠および上下架料ならびに船舶の移動に要する費用は、全額認容する。 | 　入出渠および上下架料ならびに船舶の移動に要する費用は、全額認容する。 |
| 　船底掃除費および船底塗装費は、共同海損に認容しない。ただし、共同海損行為の日に先立つ12か月以内に船底塗装がなされていた場合には、その費用の2分の1を認容する。 | 　船底掃除費および船底塗装費は、共同海損に認容しない。ただし、共同海損行為の日に先立つ12か月以内に船底塗装がなされていた場合には、その費用の2分の1を認容する。 |
| XIV条　仮修繕<br>　共同の安全のため、または共同海損犠牲損害について、船積み、寄航または避難港において、船舶に仮修繕を施工した場合には、その修繕の費用は共同海損として認容する。 | XIV条　仮修繕<br>　共同の安全のため、または共同海損犠牲損害について、船積み、寄航または避難港において、船舶に仮修繕を施工した場合には、その修繕の費用は共同海損として認容する。 |
| 　航海を完遂するために事故による損傷の仮修繕を施した場合には、その修繕の費用は、共同海損以外の利益につき節約がなされたとしてもこれを考慮することなく、共同海損として認容する。ただし、その修繕がそこで施工されなかったならば支出され、かつ共同海損に認容されたであろう費用の節約額を限度とする。 | 　航海を完遂するために事故による損傷の仮修繕を施した場合には、その修繕の費用は、共同海損以外の利益につき節約がなされたとしてもこれを考慮することなく、共同海損として認容する。ただし、その修繕がそこで施工されなかったならば支出され、かつ共同海損に認容されたであろう費用の節約額を限度とする。 |

## York-Antwerp Rules 1994

No deductions "new for old" shall be made from the cost of temporary repairs allowable as general average.

Rule XV. Loss of Freight

Loss of freight arising from damage to or loss of cargo shall be made good as general average, either when caused by a general average act, or when the damage to or loss of cargo is so made good.

Deduction shall be made from the amount of gross freight lost, of the charges which the owner thereof would have incurred to earn such freight, but has, in consequence of the sacrifice, not incurred.

## York-Antwerp Rules 1974 as amended 1990

No deductions "new for old" shall be made from the cost of temporary repairs allowable as general average.

Rule XV. Loss of Freight

Loss of freight arising from damage to or loss of cargo shall be made good as general average, either when caused by a general average act, or when the damage to or loss of cargo is so made good.

Deduction shall be made from the amount of gross freight lost, of the charges which the owner thereof would have incurred to earn such freight, but has, in consequence of the sacrifice, not incurred.

| 1994年ヨーク・アントワープ規則 | 1990年修正<br>1974年ヨーク・アントワープ規則 |
|---|---|
| 　共同海損として認容する仮修繕の費用からは「新旧交換」控除を行わない。 | 　共同海損として認容する仮修繕の費用からは「新旧交換」控除を行わない。 |

XV条　運送賃の損失

　積荷の損傷または滅失により生じた運送賃の損失は、共同海損行為に基づくとき、または積荷の損傷もしくは滅失が共同海損としててん補されるときに限り、共同海損としててん補する。

　失われた総運送賃の額から、その運送賃の取得者が運送賃を取得するために要したであろう費用で、犠牲の結果支出を免れたものは控除する。

XV条　運送賃の損失

　積荷の損傷または滅失により生じた運送賃の損失は、共同海損行為に基づくとき、または積荷の損傷もしくは滅失が共同海損としててん補されるときに限り、共同海損としててん補する。

　失われた総運送賃の額から、その運送賃の取得者が運送賃を取得するために要したであろう費用で、犠牲の結果支出を免れたものは控除する。

## York-Antwerp Rules 1994

Rule XVI. Amount to be made good for Cargo Lost or Damaged by Sacrifice

The amount to be made good as general average for damage to or loss of cargo sacrificed shall be the loss which has been sustained thereby based on the value at the time of discharge, ascertained from the commercial invoice rendered to the receiver or if there is no such invoice from the shipped value. The value at the time of discharge shall include the cost of insurance and freight except insofar as such freight is at the risk of interests other than the cargo.

When cargo so damaged is sold and the amount of the damage has not been otherwise agreed, the loss to be made good in general average shall be the difference between the net proceeds of sale and the net sound value as computed in the first paragraph of this Rule.

## York-Antwerp Rules 1974 as amended 1990

Rule XVI. Amount to be made good for Cargo Lost or Damaged by Sacrifice

The amount to be made good as general average for damage to or loss of cargo sacrificed shall be the loss which has been sustained thereby based on the value at the time of discharge, ascertained from the commercial invoice rendered to the receiver or if there is no such invoice from the shipped value. The value at the time of discharge shall include the cost of insurance and freight except insofar as such freight is at the risk of interests other than the cargo.

When cargo so damaged is sold and the amount of the damage has not been otherwise agreed, the loss to be made good in general average shall be the difference between the net proceeds of sale and the net sound value as computed in the first paragraph of this Rule.

| 1994年ヨーク・アントワープ規則 | 1990年修正<br>1974年ヨーク・アントワープ規則 |
|---|---|
| XVI条　犠牲により滅失または損傷した積荷に対しててん補すべき金額<br><br>　犠牲に供された積荷の損傷または滅失に対し共同海損としててん補すべき金額は、犠牲によって被った損失を荷揚げの時における価額に基づいて算出した金額とする。その価額は荷受人に与えられた商業送り状により確定し、かかる送り状がない場合は船積価額により確定する。荷揚げの時における価額は保険の費用と運送賃を含むものとする。ただし、運送賃が積荷の所有者以外の者の危険負担に属するときはこの限りでない。<br><br>　前項の損傷積荷が売却され、かつ損害額につき別段の協定をしなかった場合には、共同海損としててん補すべき金額は、正味売得金と本条前項により算出された正味正品価額との差額とする。 | XVI条　犠牲により滅失または損傷した積荷に対しててん補すべき金額<br><br>　犠牲に供された積荷の損傷または滅失に対し共同海損としててん補すべき金額は、犠牲によって被った損失を荷揚げの時における価額に基づいて算出した金額とする。その価額は荷受人に与えられた商業送り状により確定し、かかる送り状がない場合は船積価額により確定する。荷揚げの時における価額は保険の費用と運送賃を含むものとする。ただし、運送賃が積荷の所有者以外の者の危険負担に属するときはこの限りでない。<br><br>　前項の損傷積荷が売却され、かつ損害額につき別段の協定をしなかった場合には、共同海損としててん補すべき金額は、正味売得金と本条前項により算出された正味正品価額との差額とする。 |

## York-Antwerp Rules 1994

Rule XVII. Contributory Values

The contribution to a general average shall be made upon the actual net values of the property at the termination of the adventure except that the value of cargo shall be the value at the time of discharge, ascertained from the commercial invoice rendered to the receiver or if there is no such invoice from the shipped value. The value of the cargo shall include the cost of insurance and freight unless and insofar as such freight is at the risk of interests other than the cargo, deducting therefrom any loss or damage suffered by the cargo prior to or at the time of discharge. The value of the ship shall be assessed without taking into account the beneficial or detrimental effect of any demise or time charterparty to which the ship may be committed.

## York-Antwerp Rules 1974 as amended 1990

Rule XVII. Contributory Values

The contribution to a general average shall be made upon the actual net values of the property at the termination of the adventure except that the value of cargo shall be the value at the time of discharge, ascertained from the commercial invoice rendered to the receiver or if there is no such invoice from the shipped value. The value of the cargo shall include the cost of insurance and freight unless and insofar as such freight is at the risk of interests other than the cargo, deducting therefrom any loss or damage suffered by the cargo prior to or at the time of discharge. The value of the ship shall be assessed without taking into account the beneficial or detrimental effect of any demise or time charterparty to which the ship may be committed.

## 1994年ヨーク・アントワープ規則

### XVII条　負担価額

　共同海損の分担は、航海終了時の財産の実際の正味価額に基づくものとする。ただし、積荷の価額は荷揚げの時における価額とし、その価額は荷受人に与えられた商業送り状により確定する。かかる送り状がない場合は、船積価額により確定する。積荷の価額は、保険の費用と運送賃を含むものとする。ただし、運送賃が積荷の所有者以外の者の危険負担に属するときはこの限りでない。荷揚げの前または荷揚げの時に積荷の被った滅失または損傷は、積荷の価額から控除する。船舶の価額は、その船舶が締結している裸用船契約または定期用船契約の有利な効果または不利益な効果を考慮せずに評価するものとする。

## 1990年修正
## 1974年ヨーク・アントワープ規則

### XVII条　負担価額

　共同海損の分担は、航海終了時の財産の実際の正味価額に基づくものとする。ただし、積荷の価額は荷揚げの時における価額とし、その価額は荷受人に与えられた商業送り状により確定する。かかる送り状がない場合は、船積価額により確定する。積荷の価額は、保険の費用と運送賃を含むものとする。ただし、運送賃が積荷の所有者以外の者の危険負担に属するときはこの限りでない。荷揚げの前または荷揚げの時に積荷の被った滅失または損傷は、積荷の価額から控除する。船舶の価額は、その船舶が締結している裸用船契約または定期用船契約の有利な効果または不利益な効果を考慮せずに評価するものとする。

## York-Antwerp Rules 1994

To these values shall be added the amount made good as general average for property sacrificed, if not already included, deduction being made from the freight and passage money at risk of such charges and crew's wages as would not have been incurred in earning the freight had the ship and cargo been totally lost at the date of the general average act and have not been allowed as general average; deduction being also made from the value of the property of all extra charges incurred in respect thereof subsequently to the general average act, except such charges as are allowed in general average **or fall upon the ship by virtue of an award for special compensation under Art.14 of the International Convention on Salvage, 1989 or under any other provision similar in substance.**

**In the circumstances envisaged in the third paragraph of Rule G, the cargo and other property shall contribute on the basis of its value upon delivery at original destination unless sold or otherwise disposed of short of that destination, and the ship shall contribute upon its actual net value at the time of completion of discharge of cargo.**

## York-Antwerp Rules 1974 as amended 1990

To these values shall be added the amount made good as general average for property sacrificed, if not already included, deduction being made from the freight and passage money at risk of such charges and crew's wages as would not have been incurred in earning the freight had the ship and cargo been totally lost at the date of the general average act and have not been allowed as general average; deduction being also made from the value of the property of all extra charges incurred in respect thereof subsequently to the general average act, except such charges as are allowed in general average.

## 1994年ヨーク・アントワープ規則

　これらの価額に犠牲に供された財産の共同海損てん補額が含まれていないときは、これを加算する。ただし、危険にさらされた積荷運送賃および旅客運賃からは、船舶および積荷が共同海損行為の日に全損となったならば支出を免れ、かつ共同海損として認容されなかったであろう運送賃取得のために要する費用および船員の給料を控除する。さらに、財産の価額からは、共同海損行為の後にそれに関して支出されたすべての余分の費用を控除する。ただし、共同海損として認容される費用、または1989年海難救助に関する国際条約第14条もしくはその他の実質的に同様の規定のもとで特別補償に対する裁定によって船舶の負担となる費用は、これを控除しない。

　G条第3項の状況の下では、積荷およびその他の財産は、当初の仕向地に至るまでに売却されるか、または処分されるときを除き、当初の仕向地での引渡時の価額に基づいて分担し、船舶は、積荷の荷揚げ完了の時における実際の正味価額に基づいて分担する。

## 1990年修正
## 1974年ヨーク・アントワープ規則

　これらの価額に犠牲に供された財産の共同海損てん補額が含まれていないときは、これを加算する。ただし、危険にさらされた積荷運送賃および旅客運賃からは、船舶および積荷が共同海損行為の日に全損となったならば支出を免れ、かつ共同海損として認容されなかったであろう運送賃取得のために要する費用および船員の給料を控除する。さらに、財産の価額からは、共同海損行為の後にそれに関して支出されたものであって、共同海損として認容されなかったすべての余分の費用を控除する。

## York-Antwerp Rules 1994

Where cargo is sold short of destination, however, it shall contribute upon the actual net proceeds of sale, with the addition of any amount made good as general average.

**Mails,** passengers' luggage, personal effects and **accompanied private motor vehicles** shall not contribute in general average.

Rule XVIII. Damage to Ship
The amount to be allowed as general average for damage or loss to the ship, her machinery and/or gear caused by a general average act shall be as follows:

(a) When repaired or replaced,
The actual reasonable cost of repairing or replacing such damage or loss, subject to deductions in accordance with Rule XIII;

## York-Antwerp Rules 1974 as amended 1990

Where cargo is sold short of destination, however, it shall contribute upon the actual net proceeds of sale, with the addition of any amount made good as general average.

Passengers' luggage and personal effects not shipped under bill of lading shall not contribute in general average.

Rule XVIII. Damage to Ship
The amount to be allowed as general average for damage or loss to the ship, her machinery and/or gear caused by a general average act shall be as follows:

(a) When repaired or replaced,
The actual reasonable cost of repairing or replacing such damage or loss, subject to deductions in accordance with Rule XIII;

| 1994年ヨーク・アントワープ規則 | 1990年修正<br>1974年ヨーク・アントワープ規則 |
|---|---|
| 　積荷が仕向地に至るまでに売却された場合は、実際の正味売得金に、共同海損としててん補されるすべての金額を加算した価額により分担する。 | 　積荷が仕向地に至るまでに売却された場合は、実際の正味売得金に、共同海損としててん補されるすべての金額を加算した価額により分担する。 |
| 　郵便物、旅客の手荷物、所持品および旅客に伴う自家用自動車は、共同海損を分担しない。 | 　船荷証券によらないで船積みした旅客の手荷物および所持品は、共同海損を分担しない。 |
| XVIII条　船舶の損害<br>　共同海損行為により船舶、機械または装置に生じた損傷または滅失に対し、共同海損として認容すべき金額は、次に定めるところによる。 | XVIII条　船舶の損害<br>　共同海損行為により船舶、機械または装置に生じた損傷または滅失に対し、共同海損として認容すべき金額は、次に定めるところによる。 |
| 　(a)　修繕または新替された場合<br>　損傷または滅失を修繕または新替するのに実際に要した合理的な費用。ただし、XIII条による控除を行う。 | 　(a)　修繕または新替された場合<br>　損傷または滅失を修繕または新替するのに実際に要した合理的な費用。ただし、XIII条による控除を行う。 |

## York-Antwerp Rules 1994

(b) When not repaired or replaced,

The reasonable depreciation arising from such damage or loss, but not exceeding the estimated cost of repairs. But where the ship is an actual total loss or when the cost of repairs of the damage would exceed the value of the ship when repaired, the amount to be allowed as general average shall be the difference between the estimated sound value of the ship after deducting therefrom the estimated cost of repairing damage which is not general average and the value of the ship in her damaged state which may be measured by the net proceeds of sale, if any.

### Rule XIX. Undeclared or Wrongfully Declared Cargo

Damage or loss caused to goods loaded without the knowledge of the shipowner or his agent or to goods wilfully misdescribed at time of shipment shall not be allowed as general average, but such goods shall remain liable to contribute, if saved.

## York-Antwerp Rules 1974 as amended 1990

(b) When not repaired or replaced,

The reasonable depreciation arising from such damage or loss, but not exceeding the estimated cost of repairs. But where the ship is an actual total loss or when the cost of repairs of the damage would exceed the value of the ship when repaired, the amount to be allowed as general average shall be the difference between the estimated sound value of the ship after deducting therefrom the estimated cost of repairing damage which is not general average and the value of the ship in her damaged state which may be measured by the net proceeds of sale, if any.

### Rule XIX. Undeclared or Wrongfully Declared Cargo

Damage or loss caused to goods loaded without the knowledge of the shipowner or his agent or to goods wilfully misdescribed at time of shipment shall not be allowed as general average, but such goods shall remain liable to contribute, if saved.

## 1994年ヨーク・アントワープ規則

(b) 修繕または新替されなかった場合

その損傷または滅失に起因する合理的な減価額。ただし、修繕費の見積額を超えないものとする。船舶が現実全損となった場合、または損傷の修繕費が修繕後の船価を超過すると思われる場合には、共同海損として認容する額は、船舶の正体価額の見積額から共同海損でない損傷の修繕費の見積額を控除した価額と、もし売却された場合には正味売得金により算定することができる船舶の損傷価額との差額とする。

### XIX条 不申告または不正申告の積荷

船主もしくはその代理人に無断で積込んだ積荷、または船積みに際して故意に不正表示した積荷に生じた損傷または滅失は、共同海損として認容しない。ただし、その積荷が保存されたときは、共同海損を分担すべき責めを負う。

## 1990年修正
## 1974年ヨーク・アントワープ規則

(b) 修繕または新替されなかった場合

その損傷または滅失に起因する合理的な減価額。ただし、修繕費の見積額を超えないものとする。船舶が現実全損となった場合、または損傷の修繕費が修繕後の船価を超過すると思われる場合には、共同海損として認容する額は、船舶の正体価額の見積額から共同海損でない損傷の修繕費の見積額を控除した価額と、もし売却された場合には正味売得金により算定することができる船舶の損傷価額との差額とする。

### XIX条 不申告または不正申告の積荷

船主もしくはその代理人に無断で積込んだ積荷、または船積みに際して故意に不正表示した積荷に生じた損傷または滅失は、共同海損として認容しない。ただし、その積荷が保存されたときは、共同海損を分担すべき責めを負う。

| York-Antwerp Rules 1994 | York-Antwerp Rules 1974 as amended 1990 |
|---|---|
| Damage or loss caused to goods which have been wrongfully declared on shipment at a value which is lower than their real value shall be contributed for at the declared value, but such goods shall contribute upon their actual value. | Damage or loss caused to goods which have been wrongfully declared on shipment at a value which is lower than their real value shall be contributed for at the declared value, but such goods shall contribute upon thier actual value. |
| **Rule XX. Provision of Funds** A commission of 2 per cent on general average disbursements, other than the wages and maintenance of master, officers and crew and fuel and stores not replaced during the voyage, shall be allowed in general average. | **Rule XX. Provision of Funds** A commission of 2 per cent on general average disbursements, other than the wages and maintenance of master, officers and crew and fuel and stores not replaced during the voyage, shall be allowed in general average, but when the funds are not provided by any of the contributing interests, the necessary cost of obtaining the funds required by means of a bottomry bond or otherwise, or the loss sustained by owners of goods sold for the purpose, shall be allowed in general average. |
| **The capital** loss sustained by the owners of goods sold for the purpose **of raising funds to defray general average disbursements** shall be allowed in general average. | |
| The cost of insuring general average disbursements shall also be **admitted** in general average. | The cost of insuring money advanced to pay for general average disbursements shall also be allowed in general average. |

## 1994年ヨーク・アントワープ規則

　船積みに際し、その真実の価額より低い価額で不正申告した積荷に生じた損傷または滅失は、その申告価額に基づいて認容する。ただし、その積荷はその実際の価額により分担する。

### XX条　資金の供給

　共同海損支出のうち、船長、職員および部員の給料および扶養料、ならびにその航海中に補給しなかった燃料および貯蔵品以外のものについては、2％の立替手数料を共同海損に認容する。

　共同海損支出を支払うための資金を調達する目的で売却された物品の所有者が被った資本的損失は、共同海損に認容する。

　共同海損支出を保険に付ける費用もまた共同海損に認容する。

## 1990年修正 1974年ヨーク・アントワープ規則

　船積みに際し、その真実の価額より低い価額で不正申告した積荷に生じた損傷または滅失は、その申告価額に基づいて認容する。ただし、その積荷はその実際の価額により分担する。

### XX条　資金の供給

　共同海損支出のうち、船長、職員および部員の給料および扶養料、ならびにその航海中に補給しなかった燃料および貯蔵品以外のものについては、2％の立替手数料を共同海損に認容する。ただし、分担利害関係人のいずれからも資金が供給されないときは、冒険貸借もしくはその他の方法により所要資金を得るために必要な費用、または所要資金を得る目的で売却した積荷の所有者の被った損失を共同海損に認容する。

　共同海損支出の立替え払い金額を保険に付ける費用もまた共同海損に認容する。

## York-Antwerp Rules 1994

Rule XXI. Interest on Losses Made Good in General Average

Interest shall be allowed on expenditure, sacrifices and allowances **in** general average at the rate of 7 per cent per annum, until **three months after the date of issue** of the general average **adjustment,** due allowance being made for any **payment on account by** the contributory interests or from the general average deposit fund.

Rule XXII. Treatment of Cash Deposits

Where cash deposits have been collected in respect of cargo's liability for general average, salvage or special charges, such deposits shall be paid without any delay into a special account in the joint names of a representative nominated on behalf of the shipowner and a representative nominated on behalf of the depositors in a bank to be approved by both. The sum so deposited, together with accrued interest, if any, shall be held as security for payment to the parties entitled thereto of the general average, salvage or special charges payable by cargo in respect to which the deposits have been collected. Payments on account or refunds of deposits may be made if certified to in writing by the average adjuster. Such deposits and payments or refunds shall be without prejudice to the ultimate liability of the parties.

## York-Antwerp Rules 1974 as amended 1990

Rule XXI. Interest on Losses made good in General Average

Interest shall be allowed on expenditure, sacrifices and allowances charged to general average at the rate of 7 per cent per annum, until the date of the general average statement, due allowance being made for any interim reimbursement from the contributory interests or from the general average deposit fund.

Rule XXII. Treatment of Cash Deposits

Where cash deposits have been collected in respect of cargo's liability for general average, salvage or special charges, such deposits shall be paid without any delay into a special account in the joint names of a representative nominated on behalf of the shipowner and a representative nominated on behalf of the depositors in a bank to be approved by both. The sum so deposited, together with accrued interest, if any, shall be held as security for payment to the parties entitled thereto of the general average, salvage or special charges payable by cargo in respect to which the deposits have been collected. Payments on account or refunds of deposits may be made if certified to in writing by the average adjuster. Such deposits and payments or refunds shall be without prejudice to the ultimate liability of the parties.

| 1994年ヨーク・アントワープ規則 | 1990年修正<br>1974年ヨーク・アントワープ規則 |
|---|---|
| **XXI条　共同海損としててん補された損失に対する利息**<br>　共同海損における費用、犠牲および認容額については、共同海損精算書の発行日後3か月まで年率7％の割合の利息を認容する。ただし、分担利害関係人または共同海損供託資金からの内払いがなされたときは、相当な控除を行う。 | **XXI条　共同海損としててん補された損失に対する利息**<br>　共同海損に計上された費用、犠牲および認容額については、共同海損精算書の日付まで年率7％の割合の利息を認容する。ただし、分担利害関係人または共同海損供託資金からの中間支払いがなされたときは、相当な控除を行う。 |
| **XXII条　供託金の取扱い**<br>　共同海損、救助料または特別費用に対する積荷の責任につき供託金を徴収した場合には、かかる供託金は、船主のために指名された代表者および供託者のために指名された代表者の連名により、両者の承認する銀行の特別の口座に遅滞なく預け入れるものとする。この預金は、これに生じた利息があればそれとともに、供託金が徴収された積荷により支払われるべき共同海損、救助料または特別費用の債権者に対する支払いのための保証として、これを管理するものとする。海損精算人の書面による証明があるときは、供託金の内払いまたは返還を行うことができる。このような預け入れ、支払いまたは返還は、関係人の最終的な責任に対して影響をおよぼさない。 | **XXII条　供託金の取扱い**<br>　共同海損、救助料または特別費用に対する積荷の責任につき供託金を徴収した場合には、かかる供託金は、船主のために指名された代表者および供託者のために指名された代表者の連名により、両者の承認する銀行の特別の口座に遅滞なく預け入れるものとする。この預金は、これに生じた利息があればそれとともに、供託金が徴収された積荷により支払われるべき共同海損、救助料または特別費用の債権者に対する支払いのための保証として、これを管理するものとする。海損精算人の書面による証明があるときは、供託金の内払いまたは返還を行うことができる。このような預け入れ、支払いまたは返還は、関係人の最終的な責任に対して影響をおよぼさない。 |

## あとがき

　この小冊子は、東京海上火災保険株式会社海損部1994年11月発行の対訳「1994年ヨーク・アントワープ規則」を、同社のお許しを得て、英文テキストの改正点を示す青字部分※と訳文の一部を改訂して、社名変更の機会に、弊社で発行することにしたものである。
　共同海損の実務と研究のために何らかのお役に立てば幸甚である。

1999年7月1日

東京マリンクレームサービス株式会社<br>
取締役会長　中西正和

　※この小冊子は、黒と青の2色刷りで、英文テキストの改正点を青字としていますが、東京マリンクレームサービス株式会社のお許しを得て、青字部分を太字にしました。また、万国海法会のウェブサイトおよびLowndes and Rudolf The Law of General Average and The York-Antwerp Rules 第15版（Thomson Reuters 2018）を参照し、表記の一部を修正しました。

2018年12月

中田　栄一

# IV

# 2016年ヨーク・アントワープ規則
York-Antwerp Rules 2016

# YORK-ANTWERP RULES 2016

**Rule of Interpretation**

In the adjustment of general average the following Rules shall apply to the exclusion of any law and practice inconsistent therewith.

Except as provided by the Rule Paramount and the numbered Rules, general average shall be adjusted according to the lettered Rules.

**Rule Paramount**

In no case shall there be any allowance for sacrifice or expenditure unless reasonably made or incurred.

**Rule A**

1. There is a general average act when, and only when, any extraordinary sacrifice or expenditure is intentionally and reasonably made or incurred for the common safety for the purpose of preserving from peril the property involved in a common maritime adventure.

2. General average sacrifices and expenditures shall be borne by the different contributing interests on the basis hereinafter provided.

**Rule B**

1. There is a common maritime adventure when one or more vessels are towing or pushing another vessel or vessels, provided that they are all involved in commercial activities and not in a salvage operation.

    When measures are taken to preserve the vessels and their cargoes, if any, from a common peril, these Rules shall apply.

2. If the vessels are in common peril and one is disconnected either to increase the disconnecting vessel's safety alone, or the safety of all vessels in the common maritime adventure, the disconnection will be a general average act.

3. Where vessels involved in a common maritime adventure resort to a port or place of refuge, allowances under these Rules may be made in relation to each of the vessels. Subject to the provisions of paragraphs 3 and 4 of Rule G, allowances in general average shall cease at the time that the common maritime adventure comes to an end.

*York-Antwerp Rules 2016*

**Rule C**

1. Only such losses, damages or expenses which are the direct consequence of the general average act shall be allowed as general average.

2. In no case shall there be any allowance in general average for losses, damages or expenses incurred in respect of damage to the environment or in consequence of the escape or release of pollutant substances from the property involved in the common maritime adventure.

3. Demurrage, loss of market, and any loss or damage sustained or expense incurred by reason of delay, whether on the voyage or subsequently, and any indirect loss whatsoever, shall not be allowed as general average.

**Rule D**

Rights to contribution in general average shall not be affected, though the event which gave rise to the sacrifice or expenditure may have been due to the fault of one of the parties to the common maritime adventure, but this shall not prejudice any remedies or defences which may be open against or to that party in respect of such fault.

**Rule E**

1. The onus of proof is upon the party claiming in general average to show that the loss or expense claimed is properly allowable as general average.

2. All parties to the common maritime adventure shall, as soon as possible, supply particulars of value in respect of their contributory interest and, if claiming in general average, shall give notice in writing to the average adjuster of the loss or expense in respect of which they claim contribution, and supply evidence in support thereof.

3. Failing notification, or if any party does not supply particulars in support of a notified claim, within 12 months of the termination of the common maritime adventure or payment of the expense, the average adjuster shall be at liberty to estimate the extent of the allowance on the basis of the information available to the adjuster. Particulars of value shall be provided within 12 months of the termination of the common maritime adventure, failing which the average adjuster shall be at liberty to estimate the contributory value on the same basis. Such estimates shall be communicated to the party in question in writing. Estimates may only be challenged within two months of receipt of the communication and only on the grounds that they are manifestly incorrect.

4. Any party to the common maritime adventure pursuing a recovery from a third party in respect of sacrifice or expenditure claimed in general average, shall so advise the average adjuster and, in the event that a recovery is achieved, shall supply to the average adjuster full particulars of the recovery within two months of receipt of the recovery.

## York-Antwerp Rules 2016

### Rule F

Any additional expense incurred in place of another expense which would have been allowable as general average shall be deemed to be general average and so allowed without regard to the saving, if any, to other interests, but only up to the amount of the general average expense avoided.

### Rule G

1. General average shall be adjusted as regards both loss and contribution upon the basis of values at the time and place when and where the common maritime adventure ends.

2. This rule shall not affect the determination of the place at which the average adjustment is to be prepared.

3. When a ship is at any port or place in circumstances which would give rise to an allowance in general average under the provisions of Rules X and XI, and the cargo or part thereof is forwarded to destination by other means, rights and liabilities in general average shall, subject to cargo interests being notified if practicable, remain as nearly as possible the same as they would have been in the absence of such forwarding, as if the common maritime adventure had continued in the original ship for so long as justifiable under the contract of carriage and the applicable law.

4. The proportion attaching to cargo of the allowances made in general average by reason of applying the third paragraph of this Rule shall be limited to the cost which would have been borne by the owners of cargo if the cargo had been forwarded at their expense. This limit shall not apply to any allowances made under Rule F.

### Rule I – Jettison of Cargo

No jettison of cargo shall be allowed as general average, unless such cargo is carried in accordance with the recognised custom of the trade.

### Rule II – Loss or Damage by Sacrifices for the Common Safety

Loss of or damage to the property involved in the common maritime adventure by or in consequence of a sacrifice made for the common safety, and by water which goes down a ship's hatches opened or other opening made for the purpose of making a jettison for the common safety, shall be allowed as general average.

### Rule III – Extinguishing Fire on Shipboard

Damage done to a ship and cargo, or either of them, by water or otherwise, including damage by beaching or scuttling a burning ship, in extinguishing a fire on board the ship, shall be allowed as general average; except that no allowance shall be made for damage by smoke however caused or by heat of the fire.

## York-Antwerp Rules 2016

**Rule IV – Cutting Away Wreck**

Loss or damage sustained by cutting away wreck or parts of the ship which have been previously carried away or are effectively lost by accident shall not be allowed as general average.

**Rule V – Voluntary Stranding**

When a ship is intentionally run on shore for the common safety, whether or not she might have been driven on shore, the consequent loss or damage to the property involved in the common maritime adventure shall be allowed in general average.

**Rule VI – Salvage Remuneration**

(a) Expenditure incurred by the parties to the common maritime adventure in the nature of salvage, whether under contract or otherwise, shall be allowed in general average provided that the salvage operations were carried out for the purpose of preserving from peril the property involved in the common maritime adventure and subject to the provisions of paragraphs (b), (c) and (d)

(b) Notwithstanding (a) above, where the parties to the common maritime adventure have separate contractual or legal liability to salvors, salvage shall only be allowed should any of the following arise:

(i) there is a subsequent accident or other circumstances resulting in loss or damage to property during the voyage that results in significant differences between salved and contributory values,

(ii) there are significant general average sacrifices,

(iii) salved values are manifestly incorrect and there is a significantly incorrect apportionment of salvage expenses,

(iv) any of the parties to the salvage has paid a significant proportion of salvage due from another party,

(v) a significant proportion of the parties have satisfied the salvage claim on substantially different terms, no regard being had to interest, currency correction or legal costs of either the salvor or the contributing interest.

(c) Salvage expenditures referred to in paragraph (a) above shall include any salvage remuneration in which the skill and efforts of the salvors in preventing or minimising damage to the environment such as is referred to in Article 13 paragraph 1(b) of the International Convention on Salvage, 1989 have been taken into account.

*York-Antwerp Rules 2016*

(d) Special compensation payable to a salvor by the shipowner under Article 14 of the International Convention on Salvage, 1989 to the extent specified in paragraph 4 of that Article or under any other provision similar in substance (such as SCOPIC) shall not be allowed in general average and shall not be considered a salvage expenditure as referred to in paragraph (a) of this Rule.

**Rule VII – Damage to Machinery and Boilers**

Damage caused to any machinery and boilers of a ship which is ashore and in a position of peril, in endeavouring to refloat, shall be allowed in general average when shown to have arisen from an actual intention to float the ship for the common safety at the risk of such damage; but where a ship is afloat no loss or damage caused by working the propelling machinery and boilers shall in any circumstances be allowed as general average.

**Rule VIII – Expenses Lightening a Ship when Ashore, and Consequent Damage**

When a ship is ashore and cargo and ship's fuel and stores or any of them are discharged as a general average act, the extra cost of lightening, lighter hire and reshipping (if incurred), and any loss or damage to the property involved in the common maritime adventure in consequence thereof, shall be allowed as general average.

**Rule IX – Cargo, Ship's Materials and Stores Used for Fuel**

Cargo, ship's materials and stores, or any of them, necessarily used for fuel for the common safety at a time of peril shall be allowed as general average, but when such an allowance is made for the cost of ship's materials and stores the general average shall be credited with the estimated cost of the fuel which would otherwise have been consumed in prosecuting the intended voyage.

**Rule X – Expenses at Port of Refuge, etc.**

(a) (i) When a ship shall have entered a port or place of refuge or shall have returned to her port or place of loading in consequence of accident, sacrifice or other extraordinary circumstances which render that necessary for the common safety, the expenses of entering such port or place shall be allowed as general average; and when she shall have sailed thence with her original cargo, or a part of it, the corresponding expenses of leaving such port or place consequent upon such entry or return shall likewise be allowed as general average.

(ii) When a ship is at any port or place of refuge and is necessarily removed to another port or place because repairs cannot be carried out in the first port or place, the provisions of this Rule shall be applied to the second port or place as if it were a port or place of refuge and the cost of such removal including temporary repairs and towage shall be allowed as general average. The provisions of Rule XI shall be applied to the prolongation of the voyage occasioned by such removal.

(b) (i) The cost of handling on board or discharging cargo, fuel or stores, whether at a port or place of loading, call or refuge, shall be allowed as general average when the handling or discharge was necessary for the common safety or to enable damage to the ship caused by sacrifice or accident to be repaired, if the repairs were necessary for the safe prosecution of the voyage, except in cases where the damage to the ship is discovered at a port or place of loading or call without any accident or other extraordinary circumstances connected with such damage having taken place during the voyage.

(ii) The cost of handling on board or discharging cargo, fuel or stores shall not be allowable as general average when incurred solely for the purpose of restowage due to shifting during the voyage, unless such restowage is necessary for the common safety.

(c) Whenever the cost of handling or discharging cargo, fuel or stores is allowable as general average, the costs of storage, including insurance if reasonably incurred, reloading and stowing of such cargo, fuel or stores shall likewise be allowed as general average. The provisions of Rule XI shall apply to the extra period of detention occasioned by such reloading or restowing.

(d) When the ship is condemned or does not proceed on her original voyage, storage expenses shall be allowed as general average only up to the date of the ship's condemnation or of the abandonment of the voyage or up to the date of completion of discharge of cargo if the condemnation or abandonment takes place before that date.

## Rule XI – Wages and Maintenance of Crew and Other Expenses Putting in to and at a Port of Refuge, etc.

(a) Wages and maintenance of master, officers and crew reasonably incurred and fuel and stores consumed during the prolongation of the voyage occasioned by a ship entering a port or place of refuge or returning to her port or place of loading shall be allowed as general average when the expenses of entering such port or place are allowable in general average in accordance with Rule X(a).

(b) (i) When a ship shall have entered or been detained in any port or place in consequence of accident, sacrifice or other extra-ordinary circumstances which render that entry or detention necessary for the common safety, or to enable damage to the ship caused by sacrifice or accident to be repaired, if the repairs were necessary for the safe prosecution of the voyage, the wages and maintenance of the master, officers and crew reasonably incurred during the extra period of detention in such port or place until the ship shall or should have been made ready to proceed upon her voyage, shall be allowed in general average.

*York-Antwerp Rules 2016*

(ii) Fuel and stores consumed during the extra period of detention shall be allowed as general average, except such fuel and stores as are consumed in effecting repairs not allowable in general average.

(iii) Port charges incurred during the extra period of detention shall likewise be allowed as general average except such charges as are incurred solely by reason of repairs not allowable in general average.

(iv) Provided that when damage to the ship is discovered at a port or place of loading or call without any accident or other extraordinary circumstance connected with such damage having taken place during the voyage, then the wages and maintenance of master, officers and crew and fuel and stores consumed and port charges incurred during the extra detention for repairs to damages so discovered shall not be allowable as general average, even if the repairs are necessary for the safe prosecution of the voyage.

(v) When the ship is condemned or does not proceed on her original voyage, the wages and maintenance of the master, officers and crew and fuel and stores consumed and port charges shall be allowed as general average only up to the date of the ship's condemnation or of the abandonment of the voyage or up to the date of completion of discharge of cargo if the condemnation or abandonment takes place before that date.

(c) (i) For the purpose of these Rules wages shall include all payments made to or for the benefit of the master, officers and crew, whether such payments be imposed by law upon the shipowners or be made under the terms of articles of employment.

(ii) For the purpose of these Rules, port charges shall include all customary or additional expenses incurred for the common safety or to enable a vessel to enter or remain at a port of refuge or call in the circumstances outlined in Rule XI(b)(i).

(d) The cost of measures undertaken to prevent or minimise damage to the environment shall be allowed in general average when incurred in any or all of the following circumstances:

(i) as part of an operation performed for the common safety which, had it been undertaken by a party outside the common maritime adventure, would have entitled such party to a salvage reward;

(ii) as a condition of entry into or departure from any port or place in the circumstances prescribed in Rule X(a);

(iii) as a condition of remaining at any port or place in the circumstances prescribed in Rule XI(b), provided that when there is an actual escape or release of pollutant substances, the cost of any additional measures required on that account to prevent or minimise pollution or environmental damage shall not be allowed as general average;

(iv) necessarily in connection with the handling on board, discharging, storing or reloading of cargo, fuel or stores whenever the cost of those operations is allowable as general average.

**Rule XII – Damage to Cargo in Discharging, etc.**

Damage to or loss of cargo, fuel or stores sustained in consequence of their handling, discharging, storing, reloading and stowing shall be allowed as general average, when and only when the cost of those measures respectively is allowed as general average.

**Rule XIII – Deductions from Cost of Repairs**

(a) Repairs to be allowed in general average shall not be subject to deductions in respect of "new for old" where old material or parts are replaced by new unless the ship is over fifteen years old in which case there shall be a deduction of one third. The deductions shall be regulated by the age of the ship from the 31st December of the year of completion of construction to the date of the general average act, except for insulation, life and similar boats, communications and navigational apparatus and equipment, machinery and boilers for which the deductions shall be regulated by the age of the particular parts to which they apply.

(b) The deductions shall be made only from the cost of the new material or parts when finished and ready to be installed in the ship. No deduction shall be made in respect of provisions, stores, anchors and chain cables. Drydock and slipway dues and costs of shifting the ship shall be allowed in full.

(c) The costs of cleaning, painting or coating of bottom shall not be allowed in general average unless the bottom has been painted or coated within the 24 months preceding the date of the general average act in which case one half of such costs shall be allowed.

**Rule XIV – Temporary Repairs**

(a) Where temporary repairs are effected to a ship at a port of loading, call or refuge, for the common safety, or of damage caused by general average sacrifice, the cost of such repairs shall be allowed as general average.

(b) Where temporary repairs of accidental damage are effected in order to enable the common maritime adventure to be completed, the cost of such repairs shall be allowed as general average without regard to the saving, if any, to other interests, but only up to the saving in expense which would have been incurred and allowed in general average if such repairs had not been effected there.

## York-Antwerp Rules 2016

(c) No deductions "new for old" shall be made from the cost of temporary repairs allowable as general average.

**Rule XV – Loss of Freight**

Loss of freight arising from damage to or loss of cargo shall be allowed as general average, either when caused by a general average act, or when the damage to or loss of cargo is so allowed.

Deduction shall be made from the amount of gross freight lost, of the charges which the owner thereof would have incurred to earn such freight, but has, in consequence of the sacrifice, not incurred.

**Rule XVI – Amount to be Allowed for Cargo Lost or Damaged by Sacrifice**

(a) (i) The amount to be allowed as general average for damage to or loss of cargo sacrificed shall be the loss which has been sustained thereby based on the value at the time of discharge, ascertained from the commercial invoice rendered to the receiver or if there is no such invoice from the shipped value. Such commercial invoice may be deemed by the average adjuster to reflect the value at the time of discharge irrespective of the place of final delivery under the contract of carriage.

 (ii) The value at the time of discharge shall include the cost of insurance and freight except insofar as such freight is at the risk of interests other than the cargo.

(b) When cargo so damaged is sold and the amount of the damage has not been otherwise agreed, the loss to be allowed in general average shall be the difference between the net proceeds of sale and the net sound value as computed in the first paragraph of this Rule.

**Rule XVII – Contributory Values**

(a) (i) The contribution to a general average shall be made upon the actual net values of the property at the termination of the common maritime adventure except that the value of cargo shall be the value at the time of discharge, ascertained from the commercial invoice rendered to the receiver or if there is no such invoice from the shipped value. Such commercial invoice may be deemed by the average adjuster to reflect the value at the time of discharge irrespective of the place of final delivery under the contract of carriage.

 (ii) The value of the cargo shall include the cost of insurance and freight unless and insofar as such freight is at the risk of interests other than the cargo, deducting therefrom any loss or damage suffered by the cargo prior to or at the time of discharge. Any cargo may be excluded from contributing to general average should the average adjuster consider that the cost of including it in the adjustment would be likely to be disproportionate to its eventual contribution.

*York-Antwerp Rules 2016*

(iii) The value of the ship shall be assessed without taking into account the beneficial or detrimental effect of any demise or time charterparty to which the ship may be committed.

(b) To these values shall be added the amount allowed as general average for property sacrificed, if not already included, deduction being made from the freight and passage money at risk of such charges and crew's wages as would not have been incurred in earning the freight had the ship and cargo been totally lost at the date of the general average act and have not been allowed as general average; deduction being also made from the value of the property of all extra charges incurred in respect thereof subsequently to the general average act, except such charges as are allowed in general average or fall upon the ship by virtue of an award for special compensation under Article 14 of the International Convention on Salvage, 1989 or under any other provision similar in substance. Where payment for salvage services has not been allowed as general average by reason of paragraph (b) of Rule VI, deductions in respect of payment for salvage services shall be limited to the amount paid to the salvors including interest and salvors' costs.

(c) In the circumstances envisaged in the third paragraph of Rule G, the cargo and other property shall contribute on the basis of its value upon delivery at original destination unless sold or otherwise disposed of short of that destination, and the ship shall contribute upon its actual net value at the time of completion of discharge of cargo.

(d) Where cargo is sold short of destination, however, it shall contribute upon the actual net proceeds of sale, with the addition of any amount allowed as general average.

(e) Mails, passengers' luggage and accompanied personal effects and accompanied private motor vehicles shall not contribute to general average.

**Rule XVIII – Damage to Ship**

The amount to be allowed as general average for damage or loss to the ship, her machinery and/or gear caused by a general average act shall be as follows:

(a) When repaired or replaced,

The actual reasonable cost of repairing or replacing such damage or loss, subject to deductions in accordance with Rule XIII;

(b) When not repaired or replaced,

The reasonable depreciation arising from such damage or loss, but not exceeding the estimated cost of repairs. But where the ship is an actual total loss or when the cost of repairs of the damage would exceed the value of the ship when repaired, the amount to be allowed as general average shall be the difference between the estimated sound value of the ship after deducting therefrom the estimated cost of repairing damage which is not general average and the value of the ship in her damaged state which may be measured by the net proceeds of sale, if any.

### Rule XIX – Undeclared or Wrongfully Declared Cargo

(a) Damage or loss caused to goods loaded without the knowledge of the shipowner or his agent or to goods wilfully misdescribed at the time of shipment shall not be allowed as general average, but such goods shall remain liable to contribute, if saved.

(b) Where goods have been wrongfully declared at the time of shipment at a value which is lower than their real value, any general average loss or damage shall be allowed on the basis of their declared value, but such goods shall contribute on the basis of their actual value.

### Rule XX – Provision of Funds

(a) The capital loss sustained by the owners of goods sold for the purpose of raising funds to defray general average disbursements shall be allowed in general average.

(b) The cost of insuring general average disbursements shall be allowed in general average.

### Rule XXI – Interest on Losses Allowed in General Average

(a) Interest shall be allowed on expenditure, sacrifices and allowances in general average until three months after the date of issue of the general average adjustment, due allowance being made for any payment on account by the contributory interests or from the general average deposit fund.

(b) The rate for calculating interest accruing during each calendar year shall be the 12-month ICE LIBOR for the currency in which the adjustment is prepared, as announced on the first banking day of that calendar year, increased by four percentage points. If the adjustment is prepared in a currency for which no ICE LIBOR is announced, the rate shall be the 12-month US Dollar ICE LIBOR, increased by four percentage points.

### Rule XXII – Treatment of Cash Deposits

(a) Where cash deposits have been collected in respect of general average, salvage or special charges, such sums shall be remitted forthwith to the average adjuster who shall deposit the sums into a special account, earning interest where possible, in the name of the average adjuster.

(b) The special account shall be constituted in accordance with the law regarding client or third party funds applicable in the domicile of the average adjuster. The account shall be held separately from the average adjuster's own funds, in trust or in compliance with similar rules of law providing for the administration of the funds of third parties.

*York-Antwerp Rules 2016*

(c) The sums so deposited, together with accrued interest, if any, shall be held as security for payment to the parties entitled thereto, of the general average, salvage or special charges in respect of which the deposits have been collected. Payments on account or refunds of deposits may only be made when such payments are certified in writing by the average adjuster and notified to the depositor requesting their approval. Upon the receipt of the depositor's approval, or in the absence of such approval within a period of 90 days, the average adjuster may deduct the amount of the payment on account or the final contribution from the deposit.

(d) All deposits and payments or refunds shall be without prejudice to the ultimate liability of the parties.

**Rule XXIII – Time Bar for Contributing to General Average**

(a) Subject always to any mandatory rule on time limitation contained in any applicable law:

(i) Any rights to general average contribution including any rights to claim under general average bonds and guarantees, shall be extinguished unless an action is brought by the party claiming such contribution within a period of one year after the date upon which the general average adjustment is issued. However, in no case shall such an action be brought after six years from the date of termination of the common maritime adventure.

(ii) These periods may be extended if the parties so agree after the termination of the common maritime adventure.

(b) This rule shall not apply as between the parties to the general average and their respective insurers.

# V

# 共同海損に関する万国海法会ガイドライン
CMI Guidelines relating to general average

V　共同海損に関する万国海法会ガイドライン

**(FINAL TEXT APPROVED BY CMI ASSEMBLY 6 MAY 2016)**

**CMI GUIDELINES RELATING TO GENERAL AVERAGE**

---

**CONTENTS**

A)  **INTRODUCTION**

    1. Objectives
    2. Effect of guidelines
    3. Review and amendment

B)  **BASIC PRINCIPLES**

    1. Background
    2. York-Antwerp Rules
    3. General Average events
    4. Adjustment of General Average
    5. Example adjustment
    6. Contract of carriage

C)  **GENERAL AVERAGE SECURITY DOCUMENTS**

    1. General Average security
    2. Salvage security
    3. Claim documentation

D)  **ROLE OF THE ADJUSTER**

    1. Appointment of adjusters
    2. Best practice of adjusters

E)  **ROLE OF THE GENERAL INTEREST SURVEYOR**

F)  **YORK-ANTWERP RULES 2016**

    1. Rule VI – Salvage
    2. Rule XXII – Treatment of Cash Deposits

# CMI GUIDELINES RELATING TO GENERAL AVERAGE

## A) INTRODUCTION

1. Objective

    These guidelines are intended to assist in dealing with general average cases and to provide:

    - general background information
    - guidance as to recognised best practice
    - an outline of procedures

2. Effect of guidelines

    These guidelines do not form part of the York-Antwerp Rules; they are not binding and are not intended to over-ride or alter in any way the provisions of the York-Antwerp Rules, the contracts of carriage or any governing jurisdictions.

3. Review and amendment

    The first edition of the CMI Guidelines has been adopted by the plenary session of the 42nd International Conference of CMI in New York, May 2016, and ultimately approved by the Assembly of CMI.

    In order to monitor the working and effectiveness of the CMI Guidelines, a Standing Committee shall be constituted to consist of:

    - A chairman nominated by the Assembly of CMI
    - A representative nominated by the International Chamber of Shipping
    - A representative nominated by the International Union of Marine Insurance
    - Five additional members nominated by the Assembly of CMI

    The Standing Committee may recommend changes to the Guidelines as circumstances dictate, which shall be submitted to the Assembly of CMI for approval.

V 共同海損に関する万国海法会ガイドライン

## B) **BASIC PRINCIPLES**

1. Background

The principle of general average has its origin in the earliest days of maritime trade, and is based on simple equity; if one merchant's cargo is jettisoned to save the ship and the rest of the cargo, the shipowner and other cargo interests would all contribute to make good the value of the jettisoned cargo. The word "average" is a medieval term meaning a "loss". Thus a "general" average involved all the interests on a voyage, whereas a "particular" average affects only one interest. As the doctrine developed various types of losses were added to that of jettison; perhaps the most important step was the recognition that expenditure of money was in principle no different from the sacrifice of property, if it was incurred in similar circumstances and for the same purpose.

General average varied in its development in the different leading maritime countries, so that by the latter part of the 19th century substantial differences existed in law and practice throughout the world. In view of the international character of shipping the disadvantages of this were obvious, and there began the series of attempts to obtain international uniformity. An International Conference held in York in 1864 produced the York Rules, which were revised at Antwerp in 1877 to become the first set of York-Antwerp Rules.

In a modern context, as well as continuing to provide an equitable remedy when property is sacrificed for the common good, the principles of general average, as now embodied in the York-Antwerp Rules, also continue to perform a useful function in helping to define important borders that lie between:

- Matters that form part of the shipowners' reasonable obligations to carry out the contracted voyage and those losses and expenses that arise in exceptional circumstances.

- Property and liability insurers as their differing responsibilities meet and sometimes merge, in the context of a serious casualty.

Both of these difficult areas benefit from the reservoir of established law and practice that general average provides, helping to secure a degree of certainty that is always the objective of commercial interests.

It is important to appreciate that the York-Antwerp Rules do not have the status of an international convention. They take effect only by being incorporated into contracts of affreightment. The Rules are updated periodically under the auspices of Comite Maritime International, which is made up of national Maritime Law Associations.

Rule A of the York-Antwerp Rules defines a general average act as follows:

> "There is a general average act when, and only when, any extraordinary sacrifice or expenditure is intentionally and reasonably made or incurred for the common safety for the purpose of preserving from peril the property involved in a common maritime adventure."

2. York-Antwerp Rules

The York-Antwerp Rules consist of lettered rules (A-G) and 23 numbered rules. The lettered rules set out various broad principles as to what constitutes general average; the numbered rules deal with specific instances of sacrifice and expenditure and set out detailed guidelines concerning allowances etc.

Broadly speaking, the York-Antwerp Rules have recognised two main types of allowance:

"Common safety" allowances: sacrifice of property (such as flooding a cargo hold to fight a fire) or expenditure (such as salvage or lightening a vessel) that is made or incurred while the ship and cargo were actually in the grip of peril.

"Common benefit" allowances: once a vessel is at a port of refuge, expenses necessary to enable the ship to resume the voyage safely (but not the cost of repairing accidental damage to the ship) for example, the cost of discharging, storing and reloading cargo as necessary to carry out repairs, port charges, and wages etc. during detention for repairs and outward port charges.

The York-Antwerp Rules are prefaced by a Rule of Interpretation which gives priority to the numbered rules when there is a conflict with the lettered rules. For example, Rule C excludes losses due to delay but Rule XI says that certain detention expenses at a port of refuge (e.g. port charges, wages and maintenance) can be allowed; Rule XI takes priority over the lettered Rule C and such expenses can therefore be allowed.

The York-Antwerp Rules also include a Rule Paramount after the Rule of Interpretation, which states as follows:

> "Rule Paramount
>
> *In no case shall there be any allowance for sacrifice or expenditure unless reasonably made or incurred.*"

The burden of proof lies on the party claiming in general average to prove that both the general average act and the amount of any allowance are reasonable. It is suggested that in applying this rule there can be no absolute standard of "reasonableness" and that a situation must be judged on the particular facts prevailing at the time and place of the incident.

3. General Average events

The following are simple examples of potential general average situations:-

| Casualty | Type of sacrifice or expenditure |
|---|---|
| *Grounding:* | Damage to vessel and machinery through efforts to refloat. |
| | Loss of or damage to cargo through jettison or lightening of the vessel. |
| | Cost of storing and reloading any cargo so discharged. |
| | Port of refuge expenses. |
| *Fire:* | Damage to ship or cargo due to efforts to extinguish the fire. |
| | Port of refuge expenses. |
| *Shifting of cargo in heavy weather:* | Jettison of cargo. |
| | Port of refuge expenses. |
| *Heavy weather, collision, machinery breakdown, or other accident involving damage to ship and resort to or detention at a port:* | Port of refuge expenses. |
| | Towage |
| *General:* | Payments relating to salvage may also be allowed as general average in any of the above circumstances. |

4. Adjustment of general average

The basic principles are:

1. Property at risk

    Generally, all the property that is involved in the voyage (or "common maritime adventure") and is at risk at the time of the occurrence giving rise to the general average act is required to contribute to the general average losses and expenses. The contribution is based on a pro rata division according to the value of that property at the end of the voyage.

2. Contributory values

    The sharing of general average sacrifices and expenses is achieved by a pro rata division over what the York-Antwerp Rules refer to as "Contributory Values".

    The basis for calculation of contributory values and general average losses is the value of the property to its owner at the termination of the adventure. Expenses incurred in respect of the property after the general average act (other than those which are allowed in general average) must be deducted in arriving at the contributory value. This ensures that property contributes according to the actual net benefit it has received, by deducting the expenses it has had to bear to realise the benefit of getting the property at destination.

    Since values are assessed as at the end of the voyage, it also follows that the amount of contribution may be varied by further loss or damage to the property between the time of the general average act and the arrival at destination. For example, if the property is totally lost due to a subsequent accident it will have no contributory value and will not contribute to the general average.

3. Termination of the voyage

Normally, the "common maritime adventure" is considered to be terminated on completion of discharge of cargo at the port of destination. If there is an abandonment of the voyage at an intermediate port then the adventure terminates at that port. If, because of a casualty, the whole cargo is forwarded from an intermediate port by another vessel the cost of forwarding may be allowable as general average, subject to criteria set out in Rules F and G of the York-Antwerp Rules.

4. Equality of contribution

Equality of contribution must be maintained between the owner of the property sacrificed and the owner of the property saved. In practice this is achieved by the device of adding to the contributory values of property lost or damaged by general average sacrifice the amount allowed (or "made good") in general average in respect of that sacrifice. If this were not done the owner of jettisoned cargo would receive benefit in the form of money from the general average for loss of his goods without participating in or contributing to the general average losses, as can be seen from the following example:

Assume that cargo B worth 1,000 is sacrificed for the common safety. A general average of 1,000 is apportioned over the values of ship and arrived cargo (which are all 1,000). If this were between only those parties arrived, the figures would be:

| | | | |
|---|---|---|---|
| Ship on | 1,000 | pays | 334 |
| Cargo A on | 1,000 | " | 333 |
| Cargo B on | - | " | - |
| Cargo C on | 1,000 | " | 333 |
| | 3,000 | pays | 1,000 |

The result of this apportionment is that after paying their contributions to B the shipowner and merchants A and C would have property with an effective value of 667, whereas merchant B would receive cash amounting to 1,000. This is clearly inequitable, so merchant B also makes a notional contribution to the general average on the amount of the loss made good to him in general average, that is:

| | | | |
|---|---|---|---|
| Ship on | 1,000 | pays | 250 |
| Cargo A on | 1,000 | pays | 250 |
| Cargo B on | 1,000 | is liable for | 250 |
| Cargo C on | 1,000 | pays | 250 |
| | 4,000 | pays | 1,000 |

By making Cargo B "contribute" on the basis of the amount made good he will receive 1,000 less 250 = 750, and everyone is now in the same position.

V 共同海損に関する万国海法会ガイドライン

5. Example adjustment

| | | | | General Average |
|---|---|---|---|---|
| **Shipowners' losses and expenses** | | | | |
| Cost of repairs of damage to vessel's machinery sustained in refloating operations. | | | | US$ 250,000 |
| Cost of discharging, storing in lighters, and reloading cargo discharged to lighten vessel. | | | | 100,000 |
| Salvage paid to tugs for refloating vessel. | | | | 1,150,000 |
| **Cargo owner's losses** | | | | |
| Value of cargo jettisoned in efforts to refloat. | | US$ 500,000 | | |
| Damage to cargo caused by forced discharge, storage and reloading. | | 100,000 | | 600,000 |
| | | | | US$2,100,000 |

**Apportioned**

| | | | | |
|---|---|---|---|---|
| **Ship** | | | | |
| Arrived value at destination in damaged condition. | | US$6,750,000 | | |
| *Add* allowance in general average for refloating damage. | | 250,000 | | |
| | | US$7,000,000 | pays in ppn. | US$ 700,000 |
| **Cargo** | | | | |
| Invoice value after deduction of loss and damage. | US$13,400,000 | | | |
| *Add* allowance in general average in respect of jettison and damage due to forced discharge. | 600,000 | | | |
| | | 14,000,000 | " | 1,400,000 |
| | | US$21,000,000 | pays in ppn. | US$2,100,000 |

(General Average equals 10% of the contributory values.)

**Balance under the adjustment**

**The Shipowner:**

| | | | |
|---|---|---|---:|
| Receives credit for general average losses and expenses. | US$ | | 1,500,000 |
| Pays general average contribution. | | | 700,000 |
| | Balance to receive | US$ | 800,000 |

**The cargo owner:**

| | | | |
|---|---|---|---:|
| Pays general average contribution. | US$ | | 1,400,000 |
| Receives credit for general average losses. | | | 600,000 |
| | Balance to pay | US$ | 800,000 |

6. Contract of carriage

The parties to the adventure usually make special provision in the contract of carriage regarding general average, the most common being a clause to the effect that general average is to be adjusted in accordance with the York-Antwerp Rules. Such stipulations may be contained in the charter party, if any, or the bills of lading, or in both documents, thereby giving contractual effect to the Rules.

Rule D of the York-Antwerp Rules gives explicit recognition to the fact that general average exists irrespective of fault or breach of contract by any of the parties. It follows that normally the procedures for protecting the rights of the parties in general average must be observed even when it is suspected that such a fault or breach has taken place. Equally, the existence of a general average situation does not prejudice any rights or defences that are open to parties, for example with regard to cargo damage or alleging a breach of contract as grounds for not paying a general average contribution.

The giving of general average security in the customary terms is a promise to pay any general average contribution that is found to be properly and legally due. Generally, if there has been a causative breach of contract the contribution cannot be so described, and cargo interests may have grounds for declining to pay their contribution to general average.

## C) GENERAL AVERAGE PROCEDURES

1.  General Average security

    Most jurisdictions recognise that the shipowner can exercise a lien (i.e. refuse to allow delivery) on cargo at destination in respect of general average losses sustained by any of the parties to the adventure. The preparation of an adjustment will usually take some time, so that the shipowner will relinquish his lien in return for satisfactory security. Generally, the shipowner or appointed average adjuster will send notices to cargo interests setting out what is required by way of security (the exact procedure may vary slightly according to the jurisdiction(s) involved). The usual security requirements will be as follows:

    (a) Signature to an Average Bond by the owner or receiver of the cargo.

    (b) A cash deposit for an amount estimated by the adjuster to cover likely general average liabilities, usually expressed as a percentage of the invoice value of cargo. It is usual for an Average Guarantee signed by a reputable insurer to be accepted by the shipowner in place of the cash deposit, and the insurer will then take over the handling of the general average aspects of the case through their normal claims procedures.

    Variations in the wordings of such forms have arisen largely as a result of market practices and CMI have a working party looking at providing recommended standard wordings, which may form part a future edition of these Guidelines.

    The objectives of the security forms currently in use include:

    - Providing an acceptable level of security to the shipowner and other parties to the adventure that may be GA creditors.

    - Preserving the position under Rule D in respect of defences.

    - Encouraging the timely provision of information and evidence to ensure the adjustment process is not delayed.

    Both the Average Bond and Guarantee are distinct contracts in their own right, and may, like any contract, be altered by agreement between the parties.

2.  Salvage security

    In some circumstances and jurisdictions, and under salvage contracts such as Lloyd's Open Form, the salvor will have a separate right of action against each individual piece of property that is salved, once that property is brought into a place of safety. The salvor may therefore exercise a lien on all the cargo at that place and the cargo interests will have to provide two sets of security:

    a) salvage security to salvors at the place where the salvage services end

    b) general average security to the shipowner, at destination.

    If there are numerous cargo interests, as on a container ship, interim security may be provided to salvors by the shipowner or charterer to enable the vessel to continue from the place where salvage services ended to destination, where both types of security will then have to be provided.

3.  Claim Documentation

    The burden of proof lies with any party wishing to claim general average sacrifices and expenses, and York-Antwerp Rule E includes time limits for submitting claims.

    After collecting security the average adjuster will need information from cargo interests in order to:

    - calculate the contributory value of the cargo.
    - make any allowances in general average that are due to cargo.

    Cargo interests will generally need to submit the following information to the adjuster:

    a)  A copy of the commercial (CIF) invoice. If cargo has been sold on terms other than CIF the freight invoice and insurance premium details may be required.

    b)  Details of any damage that has occurred to cargo during the voyage, including:

        - survey reports stating the cause and extent of damage.
        - the cargo insurers' settlement. (If applicable)

    The damage to cargo will be deducted from the sound value to reach the contributory value; this will determine how much the cargo's general average contribution will be. If any of the damage is allowable as general average (e.g. water damage during fire-fighting operations) credit will be given in the adjustment.

## D) ROLE OF THE AVERAGE ADJUSTER REGARDING GENERAL AVERAGE

1.  The effect of the adjustment

    In the majority of jurisdictions the findings of an average adjuster regarding amounts payable by the parties to a maritime adventure are not legally binding, unlike with an arbitration award. The majority of adjustments are accepted by the parties (subject to any Rule D defences) on the basis of the professional standing and expertise of the adjuster.

2.  Best practice of average adjusters

    Average adjusters work under different regulatory and professional regimes, however the following elements of best practice appear to be universal and are endorsed by the leading professional associations.

    2.1  Irrespective of the identity of the instructing party, the average adjuster is expected to act in an impartial and independent manner in order to act fairly to all parties involved in a common maritime adventure.

    2.2  In all cases the average adjuster should:

(a) Give particulars in a prominent position in the adjustment of the clause or clauses contained in the charter party and/or bills of lading that relate to the adjustment of general average or, if no such clause or clauses exist, the law and practice obtaining at the place where the adventure ends. Where conflicting provisions exist, the adjuster should explain in appropriate detail the reason for the basis of adjustment chosen.

(b) Set out the facts that give rise to the general average.

(c) Where the York-Antwerp Rules apply, identify the lettered and/or numbered Rules that are relied upon in making the allowances in the adjustment.

(d) Explain in appropriate detail the choice of currency in which the adjustment is based.

(e) Make appropriate enquiries as to whether any recovery relating to the casualty is being undertaken, and set out the results of those enquiries in the adjustment.

2.3  On request, and when practicable, the adjuster should make available copies of reports and invoices relied upon in the preparation of the adjustment.

### E) ROLE OF THE GENERAL INTEREST SURVEYOR

The "General Interest" or "G.A. Surveyor" may be appointed by the Shipowners on behalf of all parties involved in the common maritime adventure, usually only in the larger casualties or where cargo sacrifices are likely to be involved. The Shipowner is responsible for settlement of the G.A. Surveyor's charges, which are allowed as General Average, but the G.A. surveyor is expected to act in an independent and impartial manner when recording the facts and making recommendations.

The G.A. Surveyor's role is not to investigate the circumstances leading up to a general average situation (e.g. the cause of a fire) but once the situation exists, his role is generally as follows:

1) To advise all parties on the steps necessary to ensure the common safety of ship and cargo.

2) To monitor the steps actually taken by the parties to ensure that proper regard is taken of the General Interest.

3) To review General Average expenditure incurred and advise the Adjusters as to whether the costs are fair and reasonable.

4) To identify and quantify any General Average sacrifice of ship or cargo.

5) To ensure that General Average damage is minimized wherever possible i.e. by reconditioning or sale of damaged cargo. Except in cases of extreme urgency or where communications are difficult, any significant action with regard to cargo (e.g. arranging for its sale at a Port of Refuge) must be taken in consultation with the concerned in cargo.

2. The authority and funds to make disbursements will generally come from the Shipowner, usually via the Master or the Local Agents. The G.A. Surveyor therefore has no authority to order any particular course of action and his role is an advisory one. However, the G.A. Surveyor's impartial position and his influence on the eventual treatment of the expenditure will give his advice considerable weight with the other parties involved.

3. The G.A. Surveyor should also be aware that several other Surveyors may be in attendance on behalf of particular interests and that, for reasons of economy, duplication of reporting should be avoided. In the event of any doubt arising as to the depth of investigation required from the G.A. Surveyor, the Adjuster should be contacted for guidance. The G.A. Surveyor is effectively appointed to act on behalf of the whole General Average community, any of whom are generally entitled to view all his exchanges of correspondence and reports.

V　共同海損に関する万国海法会ガイドライン

**F)** **YORK-ANTWERP RULES 2016**

1. Rule VI - Salvage

    The wording of Rule VI paragraph (b) is new to the York Antwerp Rules 2016. It arises from concerns that, if the ship and cargo have already paid salvage separately (for example under Lloyd's Open Form) based on salved values (at termination of the salvors' services), allowing salvage as general average and re-apportioning it over contributory values (at destination) may give rise to additional cost and delays, while making no significant difference to the proportion payable by each party.

    A variety of measures to meet these concerns have been considered, ranging from complete exclusion of salvage to using a fixed percentage mechanism. Such measures were found, during extensive CMI discussions to produce inequitable results or were impossible to apply across the range of cases encountered in practice.

    It was pointed out that many leading adjusters will, when appropriate, propose to the parties that if re-apportionment of salvage as general average will not produce a meaningful change in the figures or will be disproportionately costly, the salvage should be omitted from the adjustment; it is then up to the parties to decide whether it should be included or not. However, it was considered that a means should be found to make this practice more universal and to set out express criteria that would help to ensure that the allowance and re-apportionment of salvage as general average (where already paid separately by ship and cargo etc.) would only occur in cases where there was a sound equitable or financial basis for doing so.

    The average adjusters will still be required to exercise their professional judgement in applying paragraph (b) because several of the criteria (i-v) that are listed require a view to be taken as to what should be deemed to be "significant" in the context of a particular case. Because of the wide range of cases that the York-Antwerp Rules apply to, it was not considered desirable to offer a fixed definition of how "significant" should be construed, other than to note that the objective of the new clause was to reduce the time and cost of the adjustment process where it is possible to do so.

    When assessing whether there is a significant difference between settlements and awards for the purposes of Rule VI(b)(v) the adjuster should have regard only to the basic award or settlement against all salved interests before currency adjustment, interest, cost of collecting security and all parties' legal costs.

2. Rule XXII – Treatment of Cash Deposits

    Under Rule XXII(b) the adjuster is required to hold deposits in a special account constituted in accordance with the law regarding holding client or third party funds that applies in the domicile of the appointed average adjuster.

    Unless otherwise provided for by the applicable law, CMI recommends that any special account should have the following features:

    - Funds should be held separately from the normal operating accounts of the adjuster.

    - Funds should be protected in the event of liquidation or the cessation of the average adjuster's business.

    - The holding bank should provide regular statements that show all transactions clearly.

# VI

## 共同海損専門用語集（和英・英和）
### Technical terms on general average

## Ⅵ 共同海損専門用語集（和英・英和）

# 共同海損専門用語集（和英）
## Technical terms on general average (Japanese／English)

| あ　行 | |
|---|---|
| インボイスの写 | Commercial Invoice Copy |
| A条 | Rule A |
| **か　行** | |
| 解釈規定 | Rule of Interpretation |
| 海損精算人 | Average Adjuster |
| 海難報告書 | Sea Protest |
| 価額申告書 | Valuation Form |
| 火災による損害 | Fire Damage |
| 貨物損害検査報告書 | Cargo Damage Survey Report |
| 救助契約書 | Salvage Agreement |
| 救助報酬 | Salvage Remunerations |
| 共同海損 | General Average |
| 共同海損犠牲損害 | General Average Sacrifice |
| 共同海損供託金領収書 | General Average Deposit Receipt |
| 共同海損決済表 | Settlement of General Average |
| 共同海損支出費用 | General Average Disbursements |
| 共同海損精算人 | GA Adjuster |
| 共同海損の宣言 | GA declaration |
| 共同海損の定義規定 | Rule A, YAR 1994 |
| 共同海損負担価額 | contributory value of general average |
| 共同海損分担額 | GA contribution |
| 共同海損分担表 | Apportionment of General Average |
| 共同海損分担保証関連書類 | GA Securities |
| 共同海損分担利益 | contributing interests of general average |
| 共同海損分担率 | percentage of general average |
| 共同海損盟約書 | Average Bond |
| 欠減損害 | shortage |
| 現金供託金 | Cash Deposit |
| **さ　行** | |
| 支出諸費用明細表 | Disbursements |
| 至上規定 | Rule Paramount |
| 消火注水損害 | Water damage caused by extinguishing fire |
| 正味到達価額 | net arrived value |
| GA | General Average |
| GAアジャスター | GA Adjuster |

*172*

| | |
|---|---|
| GAサーベイ | GA Survey |
| GAサーベイレポート | GA Survey Report |
| GA宣言状 | GA Declaration Letter |
| 1994年ヨーク・アントワープ規則 | York-Antwerp Rules 1994; YAR 1994 |
| 数字規定 | Numbered Rules |
| 船価鑑定書 | Ship Valuation |
| 船貨不分離協定 | Non-Separation Agreement |
| 損害率 | allowance |
| **た　行** | |
| 代換費用 | substituted expense |
| 代船 | substituted vessel |
| 代船輸送費用 | Forwarding charges by the substituted vessel |
| 単独海損 | Particular Average; PA |
| **な　行** | |
| 投荷（なげに） | jettison |
| **は　行** | |
| 船荷証券 | Bill of Lading |
| 分担保証状 | Letter of Guarantee, Average Guarantee |
| 保険証券 | Insurance Policy |
| **ま　行** | |
| 文字規定 | Lettered Rules |

# 共同海損専門用語集（英和）

## Technical terms on general average (English／Japanese)

### A
| | |
|---|---|
| allowance | 損害率 |
| Apportionment of General Average | 共同海損分担表 |
| Average Adjuster | 海損精算人 |
| Average Bond | 共同海損盟約書、海損盟約書 |
| Average Guarantee | 分担保証状 |

### B
| | |
|---|---|
| Bill of Lading | 船荷証券 |

### C
| | |
|---|---|
| Cargo Damage Survey Report | 貨物損害検査報告書 |
| Cash Deposit | 現金供託金 |
| Commercial Invoice Copy | インボイスの写 |
| contributing interests of general average | 共同海損分担利益 |
| contributory value of general average | 共同海損負担価額 |

### D
| | |
|---|---|
| Disbursements | 支出諸費用明細表 |

### F
| | |
|---|---|
| Fire Damage | 火災による損害 |
| Forwarding charges by the substituted vessel | 代船輸送費用 |

### G
| | |
|---|---|
| GA Adjuster | GAアジャスター、共同海損精算人 |
| GA contribution | 共同海損分担額 |
| GA declaration | 共同海損の宣言 |
| GA Declaration Letter | GA宣言状 |
| GA Securities | 共同海損分担保証関連書類 |
| GA Survey | GAサーベイ |
| GA Survey Report | GAサーベイレポート |
| General Average | 共同海損、GA |
| General Average Deposit Receipt | 共同海損供託金領収書 |
| General Average Disbursements | 共同海損支出費用 |
| General Average Sacrifice | 共同海損犠牲損害 |

### I
| | |
|---|---|
| Insurance Policy | 保険証券 |

### J
| | |
|---|---|
| jettison | 投荷（なげに） |

## L

| | |
|---|---|
| Letter of Guarantee, Average Guarantee | 分担保証状 |
| Lettered Rules | 文字規定 |

## N

| | |
|---|---|
| net arrived value | 正味到達価額 |
| Non-Separation Agreement | 船貨不分離協定 |
| Numbered Rules | 数字規定 |

## P

| | |
|---|---|
| Particular Average, PA | 単独海損 |
| percentage of general average | 共同海損分担率 |

## R

| | |
|---|---|
| Rule A, YAR 1994 | 1994年ヨーク・アントワープ規則A条（共同海損の定義規定） |
| Rule of Interpretation | 解釈規定 |
| Rule Paramount | 至上規定 |

## S

| | |
|---|---|
| Salvage Agreement | 救助契約書 |
| Salvage Remunerations | 救助報酬 |
| Sea Protest | 海難報告書 |
| Settlement of General Average | 共同海損決済表 |
| Ship Valuation | 船価鑑定書 |
| shortage | 欠減損害 |
| substituted expense | 代換費用 |
| substituted vessel | 代船 |

## V

| | |
|---|---|
| Valuation Form | 価額申告書 |

## W

| | |
|---|---|
| Water damage caused by extinguishing fire | 消火注水損害 |

## Y

| | |
|---|---|
| York-Antwerp Rules 1994; YAR 1994 | 1994年ヨーク・アントワープ規則 |

◆著者紹介◆

中田　栄一（なかだ　えいいち）
　1961年　東京生まれ
　1983年　早稲田大学商学部（海上保険契約研究 大谷孝一教授ゼミ）卒業。
　　　　　株式会社東京海損精算事務所（現東京マリンクレームサービス株式会社）入社。一貫して海損精算業務に従事。
　1990年9月～1991年9月　ニューヨーク Shipowners Claims Bureau（現 Marsh）Mr Edward Effrat およびロンドン Ernest Robert Lindley & Sons（現 Richards Hogg Lindley）Mr Jim O'Shea 他の著名海損精算人指導の下、英米の海損精算実務を学ぶ。
　1998年7月～　日本海損精算人協会事務局を兼務。
　2018年12月現在　東京マリンクレームサービス株式会社 共同海損部 特命次長。日本に3人しかいない海損精算人の1人。


[About the author]

Eiichi　NAKADA
　・Born in Tokyo in 1961.
　・In 1983 graduated from School of Commerce, Waseda University (Prof. Koichi Otani's study on contract of marine insurance), and jointed The Tokyo Average Adjusting Office, Ltd. (now The Tokio Marine Claims Service Co., Ltd.) as a trainee average adjuster.
　・From September 1990 to September 1991 trained average adjusting under the prominent average adjusters in New York City and London such as Mr Edward Effrat, Shipowners Claims Bureau (now Marsh) and Mr Jim O'Shea, Ernest Robert Lindley & Sons (now Richards Hogg Lindley).
　・Since July 1998 has been appointed as a secretary for Association of Average Adjusters of Japan.
　・Now (December 2018), average adjuster, deputy general manager, General Average Department of The Tokio Marine Claims Service Co., Ltd., and one of three practicing average adjusters in Japan.

| | |
|---|---|
| _____ | わかりやすい共同海損　A Clear Guide to General Average |
| 著　　　者 | 中　田　栄　一 |
| 発　行　日 | 2018年12月27日 |
| 発　行　所 | 株式会社保険毎日新聞社<br>〒101-0032　東京都千代田区岩本町1-4-7<br>TEL 03-3865-1401／FAX 03-3865-1431<br>URL http://www.homai.co.jp/ |
| 発　行　人 | 真　鍋　幸　充 |
| カバーデザイン | 塚　原　善　亮 |
| 印刷・製本 | モリモト印刷株式会社 |

ISBN978-4-89293-403-2

©2018　Eiichi NAKADA　　　　　Printed in Japan

本書の内容を無断で転記、転載することを禁じます。
乱丁・落丁本はお取り替えいたします。